PAINT CRAFT

NORTH LIGHT BOOKS

ACKNOWLEDGEMENTS

PHOTOGRAPHS:

Acorn Studios/Eaglemoss 134, 140-141(b), 142(b); Applause/Eaglemoss 89-92; Ariadne Holland 84(b), 115, 116(br), 117, 127; Sue Atkinson/Eaglemoss front cover(cl), 6; Bridgeman Art Library 38(b); Circus/Christine Langley and Shirley Linekar 52(b); Bruce Coleman (Jenn and Des Barlett) 102(bl), (Hans Reinhard) 103(tr,b), 104(br); Compton Marbling 73-74; Crafts Council (Noel Dryenforth) 139; Crown Paints front cover(br), 17, 18, 19, 20(tr); Cy De Cosse 57-60; Noel Dyrenforth 141(t), 142(t); Ian Howes/Eaglemoss 26-28, 30-31, 98-99, 130-132; Tif Hunter/Eaglemoss 118; Sarah Hutchins 97, 100-101, 103(cr), 133; London College of Printing 52(tr); Modes et Travaux 20(tl), 29, 35, 45-46, 68; Andrew Murray/Eaglemoss 47, 53; Zed Nelson/Eaglemoss 36-37, 38(t,c), 93; Martin Norris/Eaglemoss 49-51, 52(cl), 54(t), 55(t), 56, 106, 108, 136, 138; Fiona Pragoff 95; William Relton 69; Mal Stone/Eaglemoss 2-3, 61, 63; John Suett/Eaglemoss front cover(background,tr), 8, 14, 34, 48, 76, 84(tr), 86(t), 87(t), 113-114, 129, back cover; Syndication International 135; Steve Tanner/Eaglemoss 22-23, 25, 32, 65-66, 70, 72, 75, 102(r), 103(tl,c), 104(t),(bl); 109-110, 119, 120(cl), 123-126; Elizabeth Whiting Associates (Spike Powell) 8, 52(tl); Shona Wood/Eaglemoss 33; 100 IdeÇs 1, 7, 9-11, 13, 15, 16, 20(b), 21, 39-43, 77, 78-79, 81-82, 85, 86(b), 87(b), 88, 105, 107.

ILLUSTRATIONS:

Carole Bohanan 94-96; Elisabeth Dowle 44-45; Teri Gower/The Gallery 137; Kevin Hart 24, 41, 62-64, 67-68, 70(b), 71, 72(t), 73(b), 79, 83, 107, 111-112, 116(l), 120(l), 121-122, 126; Stan North 12, 15, 16, 19; Jenny Rodwell 108; Katy Sleight 128; Tig Sutton 54-55.

Based on *Creative Hands,* published in the UK
© Eaglemoss Publications Ltd 1995
All rights reserved

First published in the USA in 1995
by North Light Books,
an imprint of F&W Publications Inc.,
1507 Dana Avenue,
Cincinnati, Ohio 45207.

ISBN 0-89134-650-3

Manufactured in Hong Kong

10 9 8 7 6 5 4 3 2 1

CONTENTS

CHAPTER I
DECORATING WITH PAINT

CHAPTER II
PRINTING WITH PAINT

PAINTING ON FABRIC

CHAPTER I

DECORATING WITH PAINT

◇

◇

Decorating tableware

*Give old vases, jars and bowls a new look
with a coat of paint. A few simple techniques will enable
you to disguise chips, cracks and faded colour
with irridescent streaks, sweeping curves, flower patterns,
speckles and dramatic abstract designs.*

△ *This assorted collection of glass and pottery vases
and carafes have been transformed and given a new
lease of life with colour. Cracks and stains, scratches
and faded paint have been covered up so that these
new-look containers can be used again and matched to
your decor.*

Choosing a design

How you choose to decorate your vase, bowl or jar depends very much on the shape and surface texture of the object itself and on its intended use.

Moulded and raised patterns can be picked out in contrasting colours and smooth surfaces given a pearlized or patterned finish. Colourful folk designs look stunning on large metal items, such as basins and jugs. Small vases and jars are often better suited to subtle colours and pastel shades. You can also experiment with simple techniques such as stencilling and masking.

Paints

Household gloss, car paints, spray cans, craft enamels, metallic and oil-based irridescent paints are all suitable for painting on glass and crockery as long as the object is for decoration only and does not require constant washing.

Metal vessels should be decorated with enamels or paints recommended for this purpose (check the manufacturer's instructions). All painted finishes can be wiped clean with a damp cloth without risk of chipping or damaging the colour. For a more permanent finish on porcelain, use specialist ceramic paints available from arts and crafts shops. This will be covered in the next section.

Preparing the surface

Glass, porcelain and metal are all suitable for painting as long as they are properly prepared.

Metal surfaces should be well rubbed down and any rust treated with rust killer before the paint is applied. Rust killer and metal primer are available from hardware stores and car accessory shops.

TIP	STRAIGHT EDGES

For straight edges and geometric shapes, apply low-tack masking tape.

Stick the tape in position, masking out any areas you don't want painted. Spray or brush the paint on, taking the colour over the edges of the tape. Brushed colour should be thick enough not to seep under the edges of the tape. When the paint is dry, remove the tape.

Porcelain and glass surfaces should be dry and free from dust and grease. If the surface to be painted is very greasy, it should be wiped clean with mineral spirits.

Disguising cracks

A disfiguring crack that cannot be covered can be cleverly disguised by incorporating it into the design. Paint the vase in sections, using the crack as the dividing line.

△ *An obvious crack was running down the middle of this ceramic vase. Green paint was used to cover the vase and black paint applied roughly on top to give an interesting speckled effect.*

△ *This ceramic vase had a large chunk out of the rim. The repair was disguised by the use of two contrasting colours — black and white — to create a cracked trompe l'oeil effect all over the vase.*

Application of colour

With the appropriate paints, brushes and your imagination, you can choose one of the following techniques for your vase.

Flat colour is best applied with spray paint. The colour should be built up in several thin layers, allowing the paint to dry between each successive coat.

Masking with tape and then spray painting is ideal for angular patterns. If you use a brush, the paint should be thick enough not to seep under the edges of the tape. Each layer should be allowed to dry thoroughly before further colour is applied to the surface.

Streaks of bold colours are simple and quick to apply. When the base colour is dry, streaks can be applied with a paint brush or any brush that gives an interesting effect, such as an old toothbrush.

Flowers and foliage with their natural forms lend themselves to decorative painting because the shape of the brushstrokes can be used to represent petals and leaves. Forms should be kept simple, with no detail.

Textures and patterns can be added by scratching into the colours while the paint is still wet. This allows the underlying colour to show through.

△ This vase was first given a base coat of car paint. The iris and foliage were then painted on with ceramic paints and simple, elegant brushstrokes.

▽ Irridescent ceramic colours created the shimmering quality of this earthenware vase. Broad strokes of green and blue were applied to a base of lighter green.

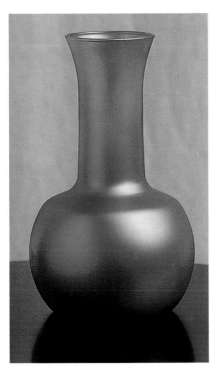

△ Opalescent blue paint was used on this simple glass vase to create the pearly blue-green sheen. A number of coats were sprayed on to the vase.

Decorated metalware

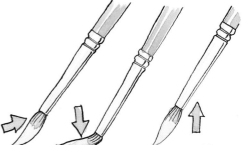

△ *Paint flora freehand. For petals with dark tips, press the brush on the surface, lifting it as you make the stroke.*

△ *Draw the brush across the surface then press down for dark centres and light tips. Move brush round in a circle to complete flower shape.*

Transform simple, inexpensive tin plates and mugs with these attractive country-cottage motifs.

You will need
◇ Metal jugs and bowls
◇ Enamel paints – black, white, red, yellow, blue and green
◇ Brushes
◇ Denatured alcohol
◇ Rust killer (if necessary)
◇ Sandpaper

Use abrasive paper and soapy water to remove any dirt and grease. Even if the metal is clean, it must be rubbed with glasspaper to roughen the surface — this helps the paint adhere to the metal. Treat any patches of rust. Allow to dry and clean with denatured alcohol.

Apply base colour to metalware. If two coats are needed, allow the first coat to dry thoroughly before applying the second. When this is quite dry, start painting the patterns. Allow each colour to dry before painting adjacent colours.

For repeated motifs such as the concentric circles, paint around smaller plates and saucers

▷ *Cut a butterfly to draw around.*

Painting china

*Decorating china is no longer a craft just for experts.
Because of the new paints now on the market, china can be painted
at home so that you can turn pieces of plain crockery into
colourful objects with unique patterns. Some ceramic colours are
'fixed' by heating in a domestic oven, others dry naturally.*

With inspiration taken from a country walk, this teaset
has been co-ordinated with the table tiles.

Materials and equipment

Apart from paints and brushes, you need surprisingly few materials for decorative china painting. Denatured alcohol and a soft cloth are essential to wipe the surface clean and dry before starting working. If you prefer to plan a design, rather than paint directly on to the china, you will need a china marker to draw on the china or paper to make templates or stencils.

Enamel paints

Watercolour brushes

Acrylic paints

China marker

Ceramic paints

Brushes

Soft watercolour brushes are best for china painting, especially if you are painting flowers, foliage or other flowing forms. If the brush is too hard, the bristle marks show up, making it difficult to get a flat area of colour.

You will need a selection of brushes, including a very fine one for linear work, and a broader brush for laying areas of colour. Brushes must be kept clean and washed immediately after use. They should never be left standing in water or thinner.

Paints

Various types of paint are suitable for painting on china. Depending on the brand, these come in a range of colours including gold and silver.

Although many paints are extremely tough and longlasting, unfired colours are never totally permanent. Some are not recommended for everyday utensils; others are intended for decorative purposes only.

Ceramic paints Special ceramic colours that can be applied to glazed pottery and china are available from craft shops. The more permanent variety need to be fixed by heating in a domestic oven. Other types of ceramic paint need no heating and dry naturally within a few hours. They are solvent based and are generally soluble in proprietary thinners supplied by the manufacturer.

Enamels Craft and household enamel paints can be used for decorating items that will not be subject to constant wear and tear. Some enamels are water-based, others are soluble in mineral spirits or a proprietary thinner. Enamels have a hard, shiny finish, and the painted china can be cleaned with a damp cloth (it will not stand up to regular washing and soaking).

Artist's paints Oil, acrylic and certain water-based designer's colours can all be applied to a glazed surface. These colours are strictly decorative and will not stand up to constant use.

Household gloss paints These can be used without undercoat, providing the surface is properly prepared.

China

You can paint any type of plain, glazed crockery or china — even tiles for your bathroom wall or kitchen table top. To begin with, try to find simple shaped pieces that are not too large. Plates and saucers are good for first attempts. Alternatively, use china 'blanks', available from ceramic supply stores and some craft shops. These plain white china pieces, specially produced for decorating, include boxes, jars, display plates and dishes, and miniature plaques for rings, pendants and brooches.

China blanks

Planning a design

Initially, keep your designs as simple as possible. Abstract patterns, geometric shapes and freehand squiggles are good starting points and can produce unusual and striking results. It is important not to overdo the design or to let the painted areas become too dense. White spaces are as important to the finished piece as the coloured patterns, so try to keep the ratio of white to patterned area the same in each piece in a set.

As your skills improve, you will be able to paint more complicated and realistic images. If you are not confident about inventing your own patterns, use an existing design or picture, perhaps taken from a printed or embroidered table cloth. Find something you like — flowers, leaves and small motifs are all suitable — and either copy the design directly on to the china with a china marker or make a drawing on paper first. This drawing can then be cut out and used as a template to trace on to the china, or as the basis for a stencil if you are using more intricate shapes.

Let the shapes of the china suggest a design — simple graphic patterns look good on clean, square shapes and more delicate floral patterns suit more flowing shapes. Freehand lines with a fine brush can look effective if carefully planned. Don't worry if some of your painting looks wobbly. You want your work to look hand done, not factory made.

Applying the paint

Whatever type of paint you are using, make sure the china is completely clean, dry and free from grease and dust. Wet colours run, so allow one colour to dry before painting a second colour next to it. Check the manufacturer's instructions — thickly applied paint may take longer to dry.

△ *No two items in this china teaset are painted in the same way. Each cup and saucer is decorated differently, in fine trellis, lines, dots and stripes. You can be adventurous with your own pattern — a consistent colour scheme gives the pieces a unity and helps to retain the feel of a matching set despite the varying patterns.*

Painting techniques
Using masking tape

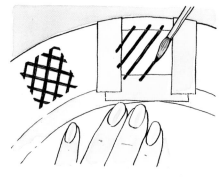

For a straight edge, use masking tape to make the edges. Here the squares were defined using four pieces of tape at intervals around the side of the plate. Wait until the paint is completely dry before you peel the tape off carefully.

Ruling a line

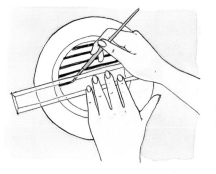

To make straight lines freehand is not as easy as it seems. Place a ruler on the raised edge of the plate. Working away from yourself so as not to smudge the paint, lean the brush lightly against the ruler and make a continuous stroke.

Lines on curves

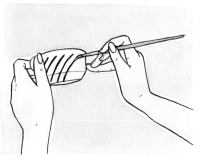

To paint straight lines freehand on a curved surface, hold the cup in your free hand. Use your little finger on the other hand as a pivot for the curve and draw lines in an arc from the bottom of the cup to the top in one movement.

Painted teaset

Leaves, stripes, squares and splodges in blues and greens are the designs for this co-ordinating teaset and bowl.

You will need
◇ White crockery
◇ Ceramic paints in blue, pale and dark green (preferably those that need firing in a domestic oven)
◇ China marker and ruler
◇ Watercolour brushes
◇ Denatured alcohol
◇ Soft cloth
◇ Paper for templates and stencils (optional)
◇ Masking tape

The cups are decorated with a triangle of blue, two leaves and stripes painted diagonally behind them. Mask off an area for the triangle and paint it first. Next apply the green leaves centrally on either side. Paint the rim and handle in the same green. When

the paint is dry, apply the stripes freehand as previously described.

The teapot has ten leaves, five on each side, and varying splodges of blue. Paint the leaves first.

The plate is best painted using a ruler and china marker to draw the intersecting lines. Then paint them freehand for a more handmade look. Paint the squares in tones of blue, then add pale blue dots to the centre of each dark square.

The bowl is decorated with a branch of leaves with vertical lines behind. The lines are filled in with neat, small dots.

▷ *In order to make the leaf and branch look symmetrical, trace the patterns given here and use them as templates or cut a stencil. The leaf is the same size as it would need to be on an average sized teacup. The branch will have to be photocopied to enlarge it to a suitable size for your purposes.*

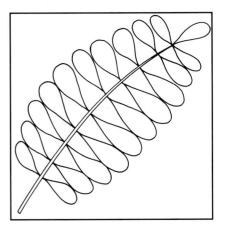

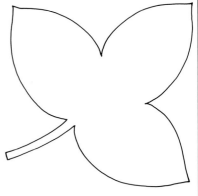

Painting terracotta

*Terracotta is a warm, attractive material that fits
sympathetically into many interior and exterior locations. Once
the terracotta has been painted, the pleasant qualities
are enhanced, rather than lost. Vases, pots of any shape or size
and lamp-bases are suitable for all manner of decorative options.*

Decorative finishes

The surface of terracotta takes paint well and can be decorated in any pattern and colour combination. You can harmonize or contrast with your colour schemes, mirror an image or repeat a motif. Although it is possible to mask off areas for definite, pre-planned shapes, painting on terracotta also provides wide scope for freehand, creative ideas.

Brushes and paints

Applying paint to terracotta is effective, surprisingly simple and requires nothing more complicated than a few paint brushes, paint and a roll of masking tape to achieve first-class results.

Once you have ensured that the surface to be decorated is free of grease and dirt, it is simply a matter of masking off areas that you wish to leave unpainted or to paint in a different colour later, and then painting. A smallish decorator's brush is fine for applying large areas of paint and any detail should be applied with a fine artist's brush.

If the items are only going to be used inside, artists' acrylic paints are ideal. If the pots are to be used outside, use masonry paint – this counters the effect of the weather and the absorbency of the terracotta surface.

The most important thing to keep in mind when decorating terracotta is not to rush things. Try to have a good idea of the pattern you wish to use and experiment with various colour combinations on paper first. If you have a sound design to start with, any creative embellishments stand a better chance of success.

Preparation

Empty any pots that will be used for plants and check for mould. If you find any, use fungicide (a commercial product or bleach) to clear the mould and then scrub thoroughly with warm soapy water. Allow to dry completely before applying any paint to the surface.

Decorated lamp-base

Using the lampshape as inspiration, this terracotta lamp-base is decorated in a way that reflects the colours and the pattern of the shade. The design combines defined lines and freehand shapes and leaves much of the surface undecorated for a pleasing, understated effect.

You will need
◇ Terracotta lamp-base
◇ Masking tape
◇ Decorator's paint brush
◇ Artist's paint brush
◇ Acrylic paints

1 Mask off the areas that are to be left plain or painted in a different colour. With a small decorator's brush paint on the first colour.

2 Once you have removed the masking tape and allowed the first colour to dry, paint on further freehand coats and patterns using a fine artist's brush for any detail.

▷ *These pots are excellent examples of the benefits of mixing planned designs with freehand patterns. All of these designs work well in their own way, from the simplicity of large areas of colours — achieved by masking off much of the pot — together with gentle curves, to the extensive use of zigzags, dots, uneven and crossed lines.*

How to plan a pattern

Bands of colour made by masking off areas, squiggles, dots and other freehand patterns need little pre-planning and probably benefit from the spontaneity of being painted straight on to a pot. But if you wish to use a zigzag pattern or do not have the confidence to work directly on to the pot, it is best to spend some time working out the position and experimenting with the dimensions of the design on paper, to avoid uneven shapes or unforeseen mishaps.

1 Create a curved pattern piece representing the area that you will be decorating by drawing around the edges of the pot as you roll it across a large piece of paper. Mark a starting/finishing point on the pot so that you know when you have gone all the way around it.

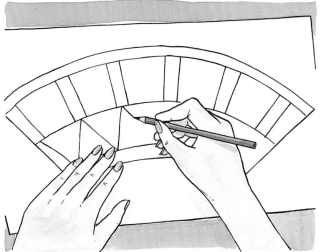

2 Plan your design in pencil, so that you can go on experimenting until you are happy that you have a symmetrical pattern.

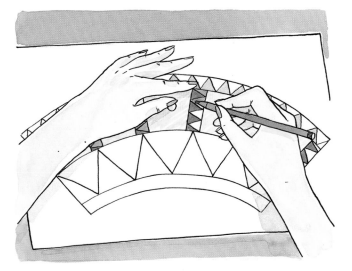

3 Play around with various colour combinations using felt-pens, crayons or chalk. The design and the colours do not have to be definitive, as you can always improvise on the pot.

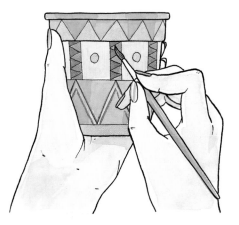

4 Copy the design on to the pot with pencil — use paint if you feel confident. To help position the design accurately you can divide the pattern into quarters on the rough drawing and on the pot.

DESIGN IDEAS

△ Discarded terracotta plant pots can be given a new lease of life and turned into a colourful garden feature by decorating them with your own designs. Here, bold motifs and patterns have been painted on to plain, pastel backgrounds.

▽ Add character to plants in the garden or greenhouse. These cheeky pots are not only decorated with paint, they have also been given features made of modelling clay — let your imagination run riot and create a host of faces.

△ Use the designs, motifs, patterns and tones found on ancient pots as inspiration to create your own artefacts. Don't worry about precision, as long as you capture the original colour and style your pot will look authentic.

Painting on glass

*Add extra sparkle to your glassware this Christmas
with some truly festive decorations. Using a little imagination
you can transform tableware, vases, and even glass
jam jars into something special and seasonal. They also make
decorative gifts for friends and family alike.*

What is glass painting?

Glass painting is the broad term given to any type of painted design applied to any glass surface. It is very versatile and can be easily adapted to your own requirements. Everything from windows and glass doors to small objects, such as vases and plates, can be painted.

For a permanent effect, which is necessary for items that have to be regularly washed, special paints for glass must be used. But, to create a purely decorative finish for a special occasion, there are a wide range of paints available for use.

Here we show you how to decorate cheap plates, bowls and containers, to create an instant effect, that is both easy and fun to do.

△ *Using gold metallic paint and some creative painting techniques, you can transform cheap glassware into an impressive table display.*

Although most paints can be removed quite easily by washing them with hot, soapy water, experiment on cheap rather than good quality glass.

Materials and equipment

Glass painting requires few specialist materials. Most of the necessary equipment can probably be found around the house.

Glass

Any glass object, from the largest vessel to the tiniest ornament, can be brightened up with a little imaginative decoration.

Textured and frosted glass will affect the distribution of colour — the paint tends to build up in the indentations of the pattern. This produces a pretty effect if the light and dark tones are incorporated into the design.

Paints

Virtually any type of paint, such as household gloss, enamel or even car spray colour, can be used to create an effective, 'one off' decoration for a special occasion, as shown here. But, because the surface of glass is smooth, shiny and non-porous, most paints, however hardwearing they are, will eventually chip and flake off.

If your work is for decoration only, and merely requires wiping or gentle washing to keep it clean, then there is a wide choice of paints to use. For items which need to be washed frequently, use special glass or ceramic paints designed for the purpose.

Glass paints are available from art and craft shops. They are transparent and the finished effect is similar to that of coloured glass. The colours are viscous and therefore do not run, making them easy to use on vertical surfaces, such as windows and glass door panels. They are solvent based and can be diluted with denatured alcohol.

Colours can be mixed together, and can be made paler by mixing with a clear extender.

You can also buy tubes of imitation 'leading' to outline your patterns, thus giving your design the look of a stained glass window. Glass paints will be covered in more detail later.

Ceramic paints are intended for use on pottery and china, but can also be used on glass. They are available from art and craft supply shops. Choose 'cold' ceramic colours, which do not need fixing by heat. The paints are opaque and include gold and silver.

Enamel, household gloss and artists' oils are fine for decorative work, but do not stand up to too much wear and tear. Use them only for ornamental objects.

Gold-striped jar

Experiment with masking tape and spray paints for the quickest results. This storage jar was covered with torn strips of masking tape, then sprayed gold.

You will need
◇ Old or cheap jar
◇ Masking tape
◇ Metallic car paints
◇ Newspapers and rubber gloves

Method

1 Tear the tape into strips and press the tape firmly in position in random stripes around the outside of the jar.

2 Stand the jar on a layer of newspapers and wear rubber gloves. Spray the jar and leave to dry completely. Carefully peel away the masking tape to reveal the glittering, striped pattern.

Other taped patterns

Use masking tape to make other patterns. Regular and irregular stripes are easiest to make, but zigzags and other abstract patterns are also easy. Or try cutting shapes from the tape — like this star patterned dish.

Leaf print vase

Real leaves were used as templates for this vase. The leaves were held in place with double-sided tape (you could also use rubber cement), then the vase was spray painted. This technique only works with flat shapes; for leaves that are not flat, such as holly, it is easier to make a paper template.

Acrylics are suitable for decorative items, but will scratch and chip with constant use. The colours are matt and should be varnished.

Spray paints, such as enamel and car paint, are quick and effective. They come in a range of colours including metallic finishes.

Metallic paints, available from DIY and hardware stores, include silver, gold, bronze, pewter and copper. The lustre is long-lasting and the paints are tough.

Brushes

You will need a range of brushes, depending on the scale and design of the work. These should be washed in an appropriate cleaner immediately after use. FEV, glass and ceramic paints are particularly hard on brushes, even when they are cleaned straight away, so avoid using new or expensive ones.

Design ideas

Many techniques can be used to paint glassware and some are easier than others. For a a quick 'make over' try using metallic car spray paints. These give an instant effect, although not a permanent one, and are fun to work with.

Some of the painting techniques can be adapted for glass painting. Sponging, ragging and free-hand painting can all be used. Sponging and ragging will give a dramatic texture and while free-hand painting may take a little more skill, results like those shown on the opening page are obtainable.

Don't overlook the technique of stencilling — as many materials can be used as the templates. Masking tape is surprisingly versatile as it can be cut into different shapes, stuck on to the glass and peeled off easily when the paint is dry. Mas-

king tape can also be torn for a different textured finish. Found objects, lace, paper doilies and even plants will all double as effective templates. Other stick-on items, such as binder reinforcements and stars, make instant templates.

Whichever method you choose, the design should be painted on the underside of plates and the outside of bowls and vases to avoid it being scratched or chipped when used.

Sponged bowl

Dip a small piece of textured sponge, scrunched up cloth or some crumpled paper into the paint. Dab all over the surface of the glass to create a random, mottled pattern. Alternatively, cover some areas with masking tape or a template to create areas of clear glass against a dappled background.

▷ *To create a festive display, fill the gold-painted glassware with spray-painted twigs, dried flowers and pine cones. For a dramatic effect, set them against a brightly coloured background; try using a blue, green or red tablecloth.*

Pattern library

Freehand painting

Scrolls, swirls, lines and even dots painted by hand, give a more formal decorative look to plates and dishes. Enlarge the diagrams here on to paper, or design your own trace pattern. Make sure the diagram is the right size for the item you are going to paint. Attach the diagram to the right side of a plate or the inside of a bowl. Turn the plate or bowl over and apply the paint to the under or outer side, using a fine sable brush. Then leave it to dry thoroughly.

TIP PAINTS

Spray paints
Do not overdo the spraying, otherwise the paint will run; it is better to apply two or three thin coats of colour than one thick one. Use only in a well-ventilated area.

Opaque paints
Leave enough clear glass unpainted to provide a contrast to the painted areas. Too much painting will lose the transparent quality of the glass.

Glass painting techniques

*The rich colours and beautiful effects of
stained glass can now be achieved at home, thanks to modern
easy-to-use glass paints. These prettily coloured
glasses were painted in a combination of five colours, using the
simple glass-painting techniques shown overleaf.*

Materials and equipment

Glass paint

Jars of transparent glass paint are available from art and craft stores and many stationers. The colours can be mixed together so there is no need to buy a vast number of different colours to begin with. For instance, blue and yellow make a brilliant green, and red and blue produce a strong violet. The paint is fairly thick, so it is a good idea to dilute it with a proprietary thinner or alcohol first to make it easier to apply.

Glass painting requires a little practice to perfect your technique, so experiment on a spare sheet of glass first. Make sure you use the right amount of paint: if you overload the brush the paint will run, but use too little paint and the brush marks will show when the paint dries.

Avoid painting large areas of flat colour. The paints look just as effective when applied loosely and can be used for textured finishes. The paint becomes tacky after a few minutes but takes several hours to dry completely. When dry, the surface can be washed carefully or wiped with a damp cloth, but it does not stand up to everyday use.

Basic technique

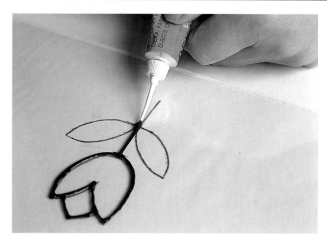

1 To transfer your chosen design, trace it on to a sheet of tracing paper and then place it, design uppermost, under the glass.

2 To copy the outline of the design on to the glass, squeeze the tube of imitation leading gently and consistently, applying the leading along the drawn outline of the design.

3 Allow the leading to dry completely before colouring it in with the glass paints.

4 When the leading is quite dry, apply paint with a small brush. Paint each area as quickly as possible, blending the brush strokes to avoid any uneven marks.

5 When you are satisfied with the finished effect of the motif, leave to dry completely. Clean the brush in alcohol or a proprietary thinner immediately after use.

Imitation leading

This comes in tubes and is squeezed directly on to the glass. It is available in black, grey and gold, and looks like piped metal when dry. The black and grey can be applied before or after the paint, but it is easier to add the gold over dried paint, as any splashes will show up on the pale outline. When decorating a flat sheet, with easy access to both sides of the glass, the outline can be applied on one side and the colour added to the reverse side.

Alcohol

Glass paints are solvent-based, and brushes and splashes can be cleaned with alcohol. Denatured alcohol or alcohol can also be used creatively to produce interesting patterns and textures on the wet paint.

Choosing designs

When designing a pattern for stained glass painting, keep in mind the fact that it is difficult to create straight or geometric lines in imitation leading. Simple motifs and abstract patterns work most successfully. Either draw your own design or choose a suitable one from another source, such as a magazine, printed fabric or patterned wallpaper.

Blending colours

Two or more colours can be used on the same area, creating yet another colour where they overlap.

1 Paint the first colour over part of the surface of the shape, leaving a slightly rough edge where the other colour will begin.

2 While the first colour is still wet, apply the second colour using a clean brush. Where the colours overlap, blend carefully with a fine brush to avoid hard or jagged edges.

TIP   **GLASSES AND JARS**

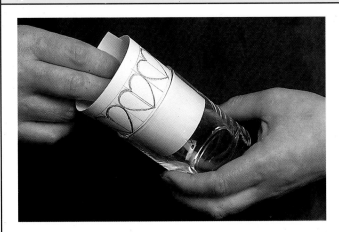

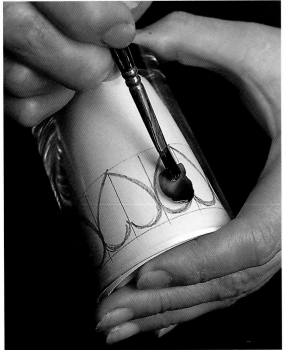

For painting regular, cylindrical glass objects, such as tumblers and storage jars, the drawn or traced design can be rolled up and placed inside the glass: make sure that the joining edges of your design match up when rolled up. Secure it in position using masking tape — it will then be ready for leading and painting. When painting, it is easier to hold cylindrical objects in your hand, taking care not to smudge the surface.

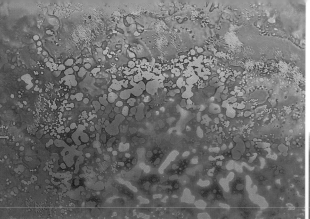

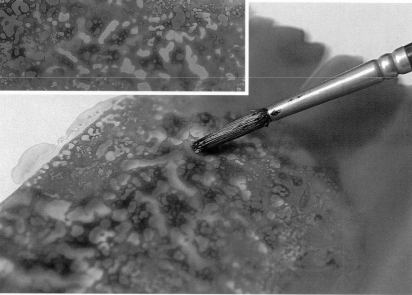

◁ The dappled effect made by dissolving paint works well on large areas.

Creating textures

Dissolving the paint

Create beautiful and interesting textured effects by dissolving the paint with denatured alcohol or alcohol. While the paint is still wet, use a brush or cotton swab to dab tiny spots of denatured alcohol or alcohol on to areas of flat colour. The paint dissolves as the denatured alcohol spreads outwards, creating transparent areas and patches of intense colour.

Scratched pattern

Very delicate, detailed patterns can be 'etched' into the wet paint using the end of a brush or a sharp metal instrument, such as a scalpel or a very fine knitting needle. The paint starts to dry after a few minutes so, for the best results, work on a small area at a time.

Painted bowl

Use both the single and blended colour methods to paint this unusual abstract design bowl.

You will need
◇ Glass paints in the following colours: emerald, chartreuse, cyclamen and turquoise
◇ Denatured alcohol
◇ Grey leading
◇ Brushes
◇ Rags
◇ Glass or Pyrex bowl

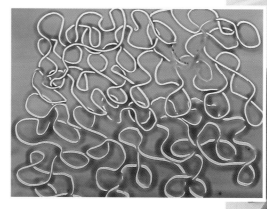

▷ The pointed end of a brush is ideal for etching a squiggly effect on painted glass — the paint must still be wet for it to work well.

When decorating with paint, leave some areas clear to create a lighter effect.

1 Turn the bowl upside down to apply the leading in a loose scribble pattern covering the entire outside surface. Leave to dry completely.

2 Apply the colour, completing one shape at a time. Paint some of the shapes in a single colour, and others with a combination of two or more blended colours.

3 Before each shape is dry, brush on a little denatured alcohol to lend texture and to break up the colour. The denatured alcohol reveals patches of transparent glass and gives the colour a mottled, shimmering look.

Opaque paints on glass

*Give a transparent surface a cheerful new
look with patterns and motifs gaily painted in opaque colours.
Ceramic paints look terrific applied to glassware,
as they have a glossy, opaque appearance, and they also offer
the advantage of a permanent finish.*

Many types of paint can be used for painting on glassware for a purely decorative effect. But, for a more permanent finish, use ceramic craft paints; available in a wide range of colours, they are ideal for achieving a glossy, opaque finish. Opaque paints, unlike transparent paints, do not allow light to pass through them; this enables you to create areas of bold, solid colour which successfully contrast with the transparent surface of the glass.

Materials and equipment

Ceramic paints Some ceramic paints dry naturally, but others must be baked in a domestic oven. Colours fixed by heating are generally tougher than the self-drying ones. Since glassware cracks if it is overheated or exposed to sudden changes of temperature, we took the precaution of putting the glasses in the oven before turning up the heat. A final cost of ceramic varnish makes the paint more permanent.

△ *With just a little ingenuity, some opaque paints and a simple but effective flower design, you can transform inexpensive, plain glass plates into a stylish tea-set to add sparkle to a summer picnic.*

Alternative paints For purely decorative purposes, craft enamels, domestic gloss, car spray paints or artists' oils and acrylics all work well. (For more information, see pages 21-24.)

Paint brushes in a range of sizes are essential for painting freehand designs on glass.

Diffusers are useful for applying paint, to achieve a smooth, even finish. For more information about diffusers see page 106.

Glass surfaces Any glass surface, including frosted glass, can be decorated. As well as jars and vases, door panels and mirrors can also be painted. Obviously, when using the variety of paints that need to be heat-fixed, the glass item must be small enough to fit into an oven. It may be possible to remove small panes and panels from their setting for this purpose; but it is generally easier to use the less permanent paints and to take extra care when cleaning the glass.

You will also need masking tape, paper to protect the work surface and a **pair of sharp scissors.**

Using masking tape

For stripy patterns, simply press the masking tape firmly on to the glass in the desired design and apply the paint, either by spraying or with a brush. Ordinary spray paint was used for this demonstration; for a more permanent finish, use ceramic paints and, for a smoother finish, apply them with a diffuser.

1 Press the masking tape firmly on to the areas you do not want painted.

Freehand painting

Freehand painting with a brush works well on any glass surface. Here, a fine sable brush is used to paint a simple flower motif on a glass tumbler. A bigger brush would achieve a similar result, suitable for a larger area.

Whether you are painting a small glass or a large panel, the secret is to choose a subject which lends itself to the technique; avoid anything too precise or geometric in shape. Natural patterns, such as those found adorning flowers, plants, birds and fish are all ideal subjects for freehand brush painting, but always keep the subject being painted as simple as possible.

1 For very loose designs, you can paint directly on to the glass without using a drawing as a guide. Otherwise, it is a good idea to make a simple drawing of your design. If painting a flat sheet of glass, place the drawing under the glass. For a tumbler, jug or other container, roll the drawing up and place it inside. Secure with tape.

2 Following the lines of the design, paint the main colours first. Use golden yellow paint to fill in the flower petals.

3 Add the leaves, using light green paint. Do not worry if the leaves are slightly different from the drawing — you will find that the shapes of the brush strokes make very good leaves.

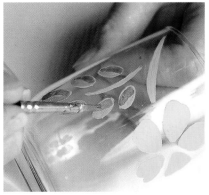

4 Then make simple, effective shadows for the petals and leaves by using a darker version of the first colour. For instance, a stroke of dark green on the pale green leaf adds a touch of realism and turns a flat green shape into a convincing 'leaf'.

5 A dab of orange on the inner tip of each yellow petal also helps to bring the flower to life. Allow the paint to dry completely before fixing it according to the manufacturer's instructions.

2 If you are using a diffuser or spray paint, make sure that the surrounding area is well protected from the paint and also that the room is well ventilated. Apply the paint in short, light bursts, gradually building up the paint in thin layers. Too much paint in one place will cause ugly runs and spoil the finished effect.

3 Leave the paint to dry thoroughly and then carefully remove the masking tape. Fix the paint according to the manufacturer's instructions.

Repeat patterns

When painting borders and repeat patterns it saves both time and effort to prepare a cut-out mask from a piece of folded paper. This technique can be used for borders on flat panes of glass or for 'all-round' patterns on glass jugs, jars and vases. Simple abstract shapes are easy to work and look especially effective on small glass objects, such as tumblers; but larger items — such as door or window panes, mirrors, or even the glass on a picture frame — offer greater freedom to be more ambitious with designs.

1 Cut a length of paper to the width you require for the mask — in this case, to the depth of the glass tumbler. Fold the paper into pleats, creasing each fold firmly so that it will open out like a concertina. The narrower the pleats, the smaller the finished design will be. For larger repeat patterns make wider pleats in the paper.

2 If necessary, draw the pattern on the folded paper first. Then make the mask by cutting right through all the pleated layers with scissors or a sharp scalpel.

4 Use masking tape to protect the bottom of the glass tumbler from getting covered in splatters of excess paint; cover the work surface with newspaper. Turning the glass round as you work, spray the paint in thin layers, building up the colour gradually. Too much paint in one place will cause drips and spoil the finished effect.

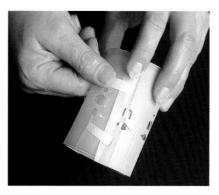

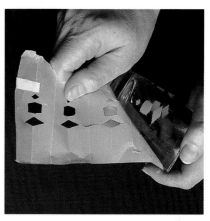

3 Unfold the paper and stretch it round the tumbler, taping it firmly in place. If the paper is very creased, iron it first.

5 Wait until the paint is dry before removing the mask. Fix the paint according to the manufacturer's instructions.

Party glasses

You will need
◇ Plain tumblers
◇ Masking tape
◇ Diffuser
◇ Ceramic paints (heat-fixed)

Method

1 Mask out the areas that are not to be painted with the masking tape, making sure the edges of the tape are pressed firmly down. Stripes can vary in width and can

also run horizontally, vertically or diagonally.

2 Ceramic colours may need to be diluted slightly if being used with the diffuser. Most paints are diluted with water, but some may need a special solvent, so follow the manufacturer's instructions. Build up the colour in thin layers, leave to dry and then remove the tape taking care not to remove any paint.

△ *Masking tape and ceramic paints can be quickly and easily used to make bright and cheerful glasses. They are ideal for a children's party — a stripy straw and a slice of lemon add the finishing touch.*

3 Place the glasses in an oven. Fix the colours by heating to a temperature of 390°F (200°C); Gas 6 for 30 minutes, or follow the manufacturer's instructions.

Painting papier mâché

*Using a variety of paints, pens and
pastel crayons in simple, colourful designs, it is possible to
create glorious decorative effects on papier
mâché objects. They make gorgeous ornaments for the home or
stylish presents to give to friends.*

Papier mâché objects are easy to make using a variety of techniques. Once you have made your papier mâché item, it must be primed with emulsion paint, to provide a smooth surface on which to work a colourful design. Almost any type of paint, pens or pastel crayons can be used to create stunning decorative patterns. The designs can be painted freehand in gouache or acrylic; pencils, felt tip pens and pastel crayons can be used to highlight areas of flat colour.

Finally, the surface of the papier mâché should be protected and made waterproof, using clear polyurethane varnish or diluted white glue. A layer of varnish also adds greater lustre to the colours.

Paints, pens and crayons

Base coat Colours work most successfully on a smooth, plain surface, so use white emulsion paint as a primer. The base coat will also prevent the newspaper, if it has been used to make the object, showing through on the finished item and provide a neutral-coloured base for the other materials.

Paints for decorating Most paints are suitable for decorating papier mâché, but gouache and acrylic paint work particularly well. Both are good for filling in larger areas of the design, but also work well for adding more elaborate details.

Gouache is a water-based paint which gives a flat, matt, opaque finish. Add a few drops of water to thin the gouache, to produce a 'wash' of colour on the surface. To produce stronger colours it is best to add just a small amount of water to make the gouache easier to work with; you may need to use two layers of the same colour to produce a very opaque finish. Gouache is ideal for adding subtle details, such as shading and toning, to add depth and interest to a design.

Acrylic paints also give strong, bright colours, but they may be more difficult to use as shading colours — they would need to be heavily diluted to give a 'wash' effect. Apply it in the same way as gouache, using acrylic medium to dilute the paint.

Other paints, such as spray aerosol paints, can also be used to cover large areas of flat colour, as they give an even finish and are very quick-drying.

Pens and crayons All types of felt tip pens, metallic marker pens and pastel crayons can be used to outline and highlight areas of the design. On the papier mâché items shown below, gold and silver metallic pens and brightly coloured pastel crayons were used to add texture to the overall finish.

Brushes

Use small decorating paint brushes to apply the emulsion paint base coat and the varnish. Fine artist's watercolour brushes are most suitable for applying the gouache or acrylic paint and for adding the more intricate features and delicate details.

Decoration

Use this basic technique for decorating the papier mâché to create wonderful designs using gouache, pastel crayons and metallic pens. If necessary, mix together different colours of gouache or acrylic paint to produce a whole range of exciting colours.

1 Prime all surfaces with white emulsion paint. Apply two coats, allowing them to dry between each coat. Smooth surface with fine sandpaper.

2 When dry, faintly draw on the outlines of the design with a pencil.

3 Using gouache or acrylic paints, start to paint following the design outline. Fill in larger areas first and work from light colours through to dark. Leave each colour to dry before moving on to next, to avoid smudges. Use a fine watercolour brush to paint in fine details. When you are happy with the finished design, leave the colours to dry thoroughly.

4 If you wish, use black paint and a fine paint brush to outline and pick out finer details of the design. Leave to dry thoroughly.

5 Use the pens and pastel crayons to add further decorations and to give a more textured effect to lift the design.

6 Paint the underside and insides of papier mâché items with a colour to complement the main design. Allow to dry thoroughly.

7 As polyurethane varnish will cause the pens and pastels to run, first protect these areas with a layer of undiluted white glue. Allow to dry. When wet, the glue is white, but it will dry clear. Then protect the entire surface with two layers of polyurethane varnish, allowing the first coat to dry before applying the second one.

◁ *Bold, bright colours in a modern design were used to decorate this tray.*

▽ *A similar design has been used for this brooch.*

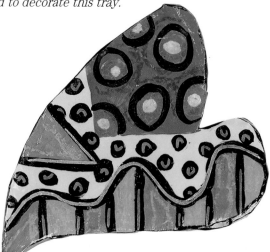

Lapis lazuli

*The gemstone lapis lazuli, with its
sensational azure colour and speckled drifts of gold and white,
is one of the most rewarding to mimic with paint.
Try out this unusual finish on small household objects to
provide an eye-catching arrangement.*

The ancient Egyptians favoured blue as a colour and used lapis lazuli to make their seals. Even in those days it was a fairly rare gemstone, and so was copied using a vitreous paste called Egyptian faience. Later, the mineral was powdered down to allow artists such as Titian to create richly coloured paintings.

Lapis lazuli with the deepest colour came from Iran and Russia, where Catherine the Great used it to decorate her ballroom. However, it has rarely been available in large quantities; known supplies of this stunningly beautiful mineral are now confined to a few countries, such as Chile and Afghanistan. Its rarity and brilliant colour make lapis lazuli an ideal subject for reproducing in paint.

What to decorate

For a realistic copy, this paint finish works most successfully on small items such as boxes, lamp bases, bowls, candlesticks and small picture or mirror frames. On larger items of furniture, use it for borders and for inlay work.

It is not essential to make a realistic copy of the stone itself. The technique can be used to create colourful fantasy effects on a grander scale for doors, skirtings, dado or picture rails, or small pieces of furniture. Old pottery, china or plastic items can also be decorated very effectively.

Recreating the colour

Lapis lazuli is no longer available in powdered form. Since ultramarine is the closest copy to its rich colour, this is usually the colour used to create the paint finish.

However, the background of any precious stone is rarely a flat colour. The depth and richness are due to the subtle swirling changes in tones, and sometimes the imperfections. For instance, poorer quality lapis lazuli has marble-like veining, which is often copied to produce a more interesting effect.

To recreate the colour and design of lapis lazuli successfully, look at photographs in books on art collections which show decorative items made from this mineral; if possible, try to visit a museum which has examples made from this gemstone. For ideas on the application of the lapis lazuli effect, look through paint finish books to see how different decorators have recreated the colour and texture using paint and glaze.

Materials and equipment

Paint

Artists' oils French ultramarine provides the nearest colour to the brilliant blue of lapis lazuli. To create the subtle shaded background, you also need a deeper blue, such as Prussian blue. A similar colour can be made by mixing French ultramarine with a little burnt umber.

A further range of shades can be created by mixing a little Titanium white artists' oil colour with each of the blues. These paler shades are used to spatter the surface lightly with drifts of fine speckles.

Transparent oil glaze

For the background, mix the artists' oil paint with a little transparent oil glaze. This gives a translucent effect, similar to polished stone. It also makes the paint easier to work with by preventing it from drying too quickly; this allows you time to soften and blend the colours. You need very little glaze — about one part glaze to two parts paint. To make the oil glaze, first mix the oil colour with a few drops of mineral spirits, then add the glaze and mix.

Bronze powder

Lapis lazuli has gold flecks in it, which are known as fool's gold because they are not actually gold but yellow pyrites. Use bronze powder, which is available in various shades of gold, to reproduce the flecks. Dip the paint brush in mineral spirits first and then the powder. Flick the brush to produce tiny cloud-like spatters, or gently trail it over the surface in subtle drifting swirls of gold.

Brushes

The size of brush you need depends on the area of background you are going to paint. A ½in (1.2cm) paint brush should be suitable for medium to small items. Use a 1in (2.5cm) size for larger areas.

Use a good quality brush that does not shed hairs; before you start, make sure that there are no loose ones left which could spoil your work. To spatter the paint, use a small stencil or artists' brush. If you want to add marble-like veins, you will need a fine pointed artists' paint brush or a feather.

Preparation work

The smooth polished finish of stone can only be copied successfully if the surface to be painted is similarly smooth. A wooden surface that is in good condition need only be lightly sanded before it is painted using this technique. But if the surface is in poor condition it is best to strip it back to the bare wood. Fill any holes and dents with wood filler, then seal the surface with a coat of primer before adding at least two coats of undercoat.

Pottery, china and enamelware need to be clean and grease free. Wipe with a clean cloth dipped in mineral spirits to ensure there is no grease on the surface.

If you are decorating metal, treat any rust and rub the surface well with fine wire wool to provide a key for the paint before you start. The surface will then need to be painted with at least two coats of primer/undercoat.

You will need

◇ Household oil-based primer/undercoat in white
◇ Artists' oil paints in French ultramarine, Prussian
   blue and Titanium white
◇ Transparent oil glaze
◇ Bronze powder (gold)
◇ ¹/₂in or 1in (1.2cm or 2.5cm) household paint brush
◇ Small stencil or artists' brush
◇ A fine pointed artists' brush or feather (optional)
◇ Synthetic sponge
◇ Clean lint-free rag
◇ Fine abrasive paper
◇ Mineral spirits
◇ Two saucers (for mixing colours)
◇ Satin-finish polyurethane varnish
◇ Wax polish
◇ Softening brush

Method

1 Having prepared the surface, paint the item to be decorated with white primer/undercoat and leave it to dry thoroughly. When it is dry, lightly sand the surface with fine abrasive paper. Remove any fine dust particles from the surface by gently wiping over with a cloth dipped in a little mineral spirits.

2 Add a few drops of mineral spirits to the French ultramarine artists' oil to make it easy to mix. Then add the glaze in a ratio of one part glaze to two parts paint; mix well. With the paint brush, paint this glaze mixture on to the surface — cover about three quarters of the surface, leaving cloud shaped areas of white.

3 Mix the Prussian blue with the mineral spirits and glaze in the same way (or add burnt umber to ultramarine to create a similar dark blue). Fill in the white shapes with the deeper blue.

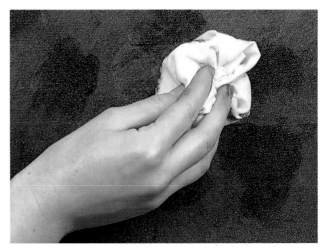

4 Using first the sponge, then the rag, dab all over the surface to remove any brush marks and to blend the edges where the two blues meet. Do not blend to a point where the colour becomes completely even. Remove any remaining marks by lightly dusting the surface with a softening brush.

5 If you wish to create a marbled effect, add the veining at this stage. To form the veins, dip a feather (or a fine pointed artists' paint brush) in a small amount of mineral spirits; then drag it gently through the painted surface to create wavy lines to imitate veins. The mineral spirits will remove the blue surface paint to expose the white beneath. Restrict the veining to one area of the object only.

6 Place a little French ultramarine in one saucer and a little of the Prussian blue in the other. Add a few drops of mineral spirits and Titanium white artists' oil to each and mix to produce two new paler shades of blue, *but do not add glaze.* The mixed paint should be of a creamy consistency.

7 Lay the surface to be spattered as flat as possible. Using one colour and the stencil brush, spatter the paint lightly over the painted surface, creating fine drifts of tiny spots. When satisfied with the effect, follow this with the second colour — but do not overdo the spattering. To avoid runs, allow the paint to partially dry before decorating the next surface.

8 Dip the stencil brush in a little mineral spirits and then in the bronze powder and gently spatter it in the same way as the pale blue paints to create subtle curling drifts. Alternatively, trail the brush lightly through the surface to remove small areas of blue glaze and then add tiny spatters of gold.

9 When you are satisfied with the overall spattered effect, leave the object to dry in a warm, dry place away from direct sunlight. When it is completely dry, protect the surface with two coats of polyurethane varnish. Then, for a really professional finish, polish with a little wax polish.

▽ *This Louis XV snuff box, ornately decorated with gold, is a stunning example of real lapis lazuli. The shades of blue and speckled drifts of gold are reminiscent of a perfect summer night sky.*

TIP FINISHES

Trial run
Before painting your chosen item, perfect the technique by experimenting first on a piece of paper. Spatter at varying distances from the surface to produce the desired size of the spatters.

Fossil effect
If you dab the surface with balls of newspaper after step 4, and before adding veins, you will remove uneven areas of paint and create a fossil-like background.

Felt tip pen decoration

*Painting dots and dashes is all the skill
you need to create effective coloured designs for furniture
and jewellery. And once you have begun, you will
be tempted to give them all the 'dot and dash' treatment to change
everyday objects into works of art.*

Instant colour

Ordinary felt tip pens, available from stationers, art or craft shops, can be used to decorate fabric, paper, posterboard, and untreated wood. However, because these colours are transparent, they cannot be used on a dark surface or to paint one colour on top of another. For more opaque, dramatic colours, use an old felt tip pen dipped in oil paint or enamel. This enables you to paint light colours over darker ones, and gives a tougher finish.

You can decorate carpets using special fabric pens — this will be covered in a later chapter.

Materials

Apart from some felt tip pens — and paint, if you are using it — you need no special materials or equipment for this quick and easy decorating technique.

Fabric pens

Non-toxic felt tip fabric pens can be bought in craft stores and art shops. They are washable, fade resistant and are made in a range of attractive, bright colours with fine or broad tips. The pens are suitable for cotton and other fabrics, including leather. Most fabric pens have to be heat fixed by pressing with a dry domestic iron.

Felt tip pens

On paper or posterboard, use ordinary felt tip pens. You can give your finished pattern a coat of varnish to make it longer lasting and spongeable. The pens can also be used on other surfaces: porous finishes, such as leather and wood, often produce successful results; on plastic, metal and other hard or shiny surfaces, use permanent felt tips that do not wash or rub off. For a permanent finish, use paint.

Paints

Oil-based paints can be applied with an old felt tip pen. This innovative approach allows you to retain the shape of the small dots, yet produces a permanent, washable finish, depending on the type of paint you use. Household gloss, artist's oil paint and craft enamel are all ideal. Paints should be diluted with mineral spirits to a thick, creamy consistency. If the paint is too thick it will create uneven dots when used with the pen.

Making patterns

There are no set rules for decorating with felt tip pens. Dots, dashes, squiggles and doodles — anything simple that creates an overall pattern — are perfect for this technique. Keep your work simple. Colour is the most important ingredient here. You don't need to be able to draw.

'Mixing' colours

Colours mixed on the palette are often disappointing. This is especially true of oil paints, when mixed colours can look heavy and dull. You might, for instance, combine bright red and yellow to make orange, only to find the resulting colour looks muddy and has none of the original brightness.

However, if you paint red and yellow dots close together directly on to the decorated surface, you will create the illusion of orange — a much brighter, lighter orange, and one that is far more in keeping with the pretty, scattered nature of felt tip patterns.

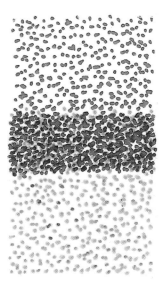

△ *Mixing red and blue dots on the object to be decorated produces a much livelier purple than if the colours had been combined first.*

△ *Orange is created with the combination of yellow and red. The tone can vary depending on the ratio of red to yellow dots applied to the object.*

△ *Yellow and blue could easily produce a very nondescript colour if put together prior to use, but mixed dots make a much more vibrant green.*

Painted beads

Use felt tip pens to decorate this chunky, colourful jewellery. The larger items are made from modelling paste or wood but if you prefer you can buy ready-to-paint plain wooden beads from craft shops. Smaller coloured plastic and glass beads are effectively threaded between the larger, painted items.

You will need
◇ Assortment of unpainted jewellery
◇ Enamel or gloss paint for base coat
◇ Felt tip pens
◇ Mineral spirits

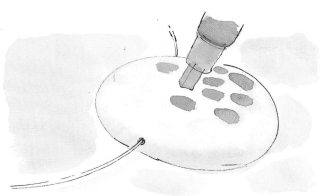

Apply the base coat and allow to dry. In this case, a yellow base has been covered in large pink dots. The subsequent colours are then used to fill in the spaces between the original dots — first mauve and green, with smaller blue dots to finish off.

◁ *There are countless colour options you can use to decorate the beads — just mix and match for outrageous results.*

▷ *Dare to be different when putting colours and shapes together, the customized results will be well worth it.*

Painted chest of drawers

Re-vamp wooden furniture with bright colours and dots and dashes. We have decorated this sideboard with eye-catching results. A similar effect could be achieved using a chest of drawers with several layers of shelving above.

You will need
◇ Household gloss or enamel paint
◇ Mineral spirits
◇ Felt tip pen
◇ Undercoat
◇ Sandpaper
◇ Primer, if used
◇ Large plastic triangle

The wood should be well rubbed down with sandpaper and painted with undercoat before being given a coat of gloss. New wood should be primed.

A base coat of bright red was chosen for this chest of drawers, with the exception of two of the drawers which were painted blue and green for a dramatic contrast.

When the base colours are dry, build up an abstract patchwork pattern in a series of small, coloured dots. The colour is applied by dipping the felt tip pen into the paint and then making the dots. Use the plastic triangle to mask off areas and to give a straight edge to each area of colour.

Eggshell mosaics

*Eggshells are cheap and readily available, but in
spite of this their decorative uses are often overlooked. Their
porous surface makes them ideal for absorbing
brightly coloured dyes, and they can be broken up and used to
transform everyday items into glamorous accessories.*

Eggshell mosaics are a cheap and easy way of decorating all sorts of items, from greetings cards to picture frames, without the need for expensive materials or great artistic ability. Fragments of coloured shells can even be arranged to make pictures in their own right.

Dyeing eggshells

The shell of an egg is a naturally porous material which allows an exchange of gasses in the egg while the chick is growing. This property makes eggshells highly receptive to the vibrant colours of hot water dyes, which are available in a wide spectrum of colours.

You will need
◇ Eggs
◇ Hot water dye
◇ Jug of boiling water

1 Make sure the eggshells are free from all residue of egg, including the membrane. Eggs which have been hard boiled are the easiest to use as the membrane is likely to have come away during cooking. The shells do not need to be whole for dyeing.

2 Dissolve the hot water dye in a jug of boiling water. The depth of colour you achieve will depend on the amount of dye used and the length of time that the shells are left in the dye. Test your dye solution on spare pieces of broken eggshell and experiment with varying strengths of dye and different dyeing times.

3 When you are happy with the dye solution, immerse the eggshells in jug of dye for the required time. Remove the eggshells and allow them to dry completely.

Coloured eggshell mosaics

Crush a variety of dyed eggshells and use the pieces to make colourful mosaics. Designs can be abstract or pictorial, like the one on the previous page which was inspired by a herbaceous border. For a pictorial design, vary the size of the shell fragments to achieve a sense of perspective, with large pieces building up the foreground in the picture and small pieces representing distant objects in the background.

Mount the shells on a backing of stiff posterboard or, for a matt effect, fabric-covered board. To protect the finished mosaic, simply spray with a clear varnish or, if mounted on fabric, a fabric protector.

You will need
◇ Posterboard
◇ Plain fabric
◇ Chalk pencil
◇ Spray adhesive
◇ Dyed eggshells
◇ Clear craft adhesive
◇ Tweezers
◇ Fabric protector spray

1 Stick fabric to posterboard with spray adhesive and smooth flat. Work out design in form of a coloured diagram; transfer outlines to fabric with chalk.

TIP	PLASTIC COVERING

If the article being decorated is likely to be handled fairly often, such as a family photograph album, a diary or a scrap book, it is best to protect the surface with a sheet of transparent sticky-backed plastic.

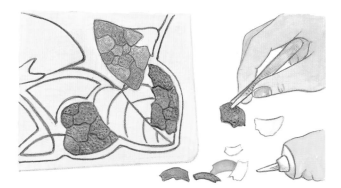

2 Break the shells up into small pieces. Spread clear adhesive on to the inner curved side of each piece. Use tweezers to position shells on to the background fabric according to the diagram.

3 Since the eggshells are curved, you must press each piece down on to the backing fabric with your thumb to bring the adhesive into contact with the surface of the eggshell. This will cause the shells to splinter into smaller pieces, but the adhesive will hold them together.

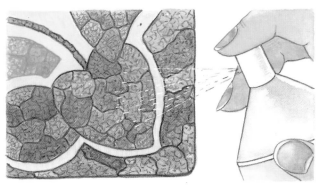

4 When all the pieces of eggshell are stuck down in the required position on the surface, spray the whole design with a fabric protector.

Natural eggshell mosaics

Another effective way of using eggshells in mosaics is to colour the background behind the shell fragments, leaving the shells themselves *au naturel*.

You will need

◇ Eggshells, washed and dried
◇ Item to be decorated
◇ Vinyl wood glue
◇ Utility knife or craft knife
◇ Flat brushes
◇ Water-based glaze
◇ Powder paints
◇ Water
◇ Palette knife
◇ Fine or medium grade sandpaper and block of wood
◇ Clear matt or gloss varnish

△ *Stylish accessories can be made by using vividly coloured glazes over a natural eggshell design.*

3 Mix the water-based glaze with some powder paint, Then add a little water and vinyl wood glue to form a smooth paste, taking care not to add too much glue as this will cause the glaze to crack during drying. Use the palette knife to spread the glaze thickly over the shells, covering the surface completely. Apply firm pressure with the knife to ensure that the glaze fills in all the gaps between the shells. Allow glaze to dry completely before sanding the surface.

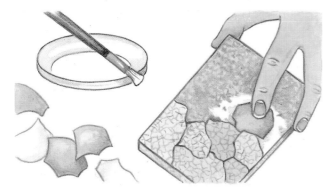

1 If the item to be decorated has a shiny surface, sand it lightly to provide a key for the glue. Brush the vinyl wood glue on to the surface and place the pieces of eggshell on top, crushing them flat with your thumb as you work.

4 Wrap fine grade sandpaper around a block of wood and lightly rub over the surface of glaze in a circular motion. This will remove excess glaze from the surface of shells, but it will remain in the cracks between the shells. Finish with a protective coat of varnish and leave to dry.

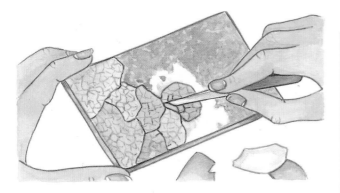

2 Use the utility knife or craft knife to separate the fragments of shell, then allow glue to dry.

TIP	BLOWING EGGS

If you need the eggshell to remain whole, remove the contents of the egg by 'blowing' it. To do this, first pierce the narrow pointed end of the egg with a pin. Then make another, bigger hole at the other end and, holding the egg over a bowl, blow hard into the smaller hole, forcing the contents of the egg out of the bigger hole. Rinse the shell out thoroughly.

DESIGN IDEAS

△ Give plain office furniture and stationery a stylish co-ordinated look by decorating them with eggshell mosaics. The telephone-shaped collage cleverly echoes the shape of the real telephone.

▷ Embellish cutlery and napkin rings with striking eggshell designs. Protect the cutlery handles with a waterproof varnish and take care when washing it.

▽ Use eggshell mosaics in leaf and diamond designs to decorate trinket boxes. For added interest, copper has been included in the design for the square box.

CHAPTER II

PRINTING WITH PAINT

◇

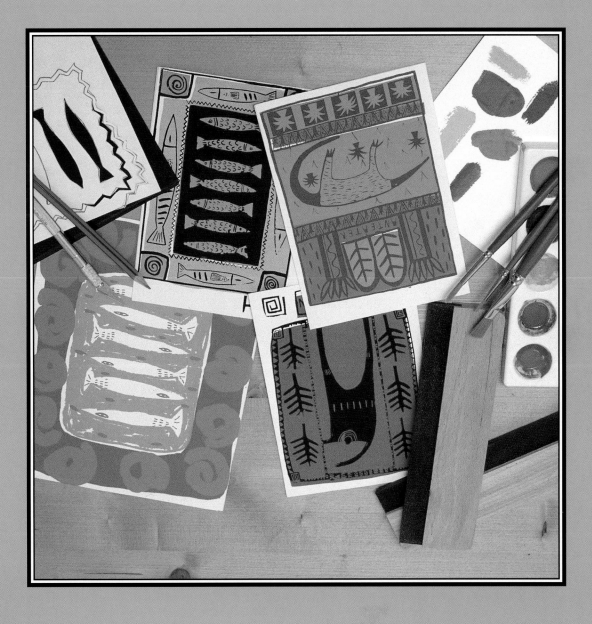

◇

Screen printing basics

*Screen printing is an exciting and rewarding hobby
that, surprisingly, doesn't require lots of expensive equipment.
You'll need a screen and squeegee, which can be
either bought or made at home. And, once you're ready to print,
the variety of designs you can create is endless.*

Screen printing is still sometimes called silk screen printing because the mesh which is stretched across the wooden frame to form the screen was once made of fine silk. Today, cheaper, mass-produced fabrics are used for the mesh.

Screen printing is used to create exclusive ranges of handprinted wallpaper and textiles, although it is now also mechanized for mass-production. Not all types of screen printing are suitable for small-scale work at home — for example, photographic printing is costly and takes up a lot of space.

The simplest method of screen printing involves fixing a paper stencil on to the screen and using a rubber squeegee to pull paint across the surface, forcing it through the uncovered area of the screen.

This is simple, quick and effective, and can be done in a relatively small space.

Screen printing has a surprising number of uses. You can make a variety of colourful and decorative items, including wrapping paper, greetings cards, posters and personalized stationery.

Screen printing on fabric will be covered in a later section.

Terylene screen fabric

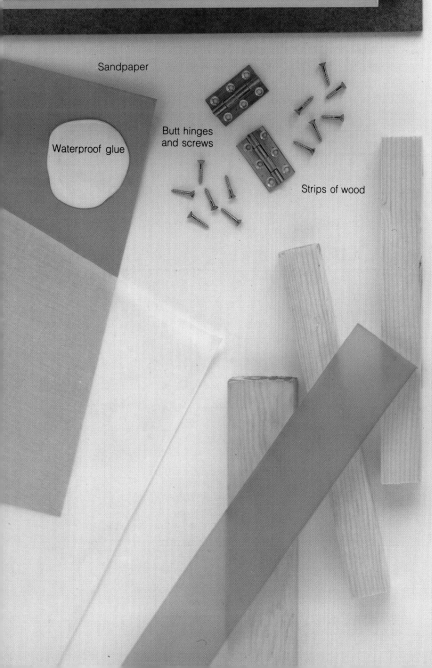

Brown paper tape

Sandpaper

Waterproof glue

Butt hinges and screws

Strips of wood

Pieces of planned wood

50mm nails

Wooden frame

Baseboard

Tools and equipment

Screen printing kits, which can be assembled at home, are available from screen-printing suppliers and some craft shops. However, if you intend to do a lot of screen printing, it's a good idea to make your own screen and squeegee to the size and proportion that you want.

Screen

Your screen should be sturdily made of wood and have a meshed material stretched over it. If you decide to buy a screen, make sure it is big enough for the purpose you have in mind. Otherwise, it is not difficult to make your own.

Tape

To prevent colour seeping round the edge of the screen, you must mask the edges of the screen with gummed paper tape or — for continued use – white waterproof tape. Gummed paper tape can be given a coat of varnish to make it more durable.

Baseboard

For printing on reasonably-sized sheets of paper, a baseboard is invaluable. This board, which should be fixed to the screen with hinges, is especially useful if you are printing with more than one colour and the second colour has to be positioned correctly in relation to the first.

Squeegee

This is basically a length of rubber fixed rigidly between two pieces of wood. It is used to pull colour evenly across the mesh. Whether you buy a squeegee or make your own, it must fit inside the screen.

To make a screen

The basic screen is made up of four pieces of planed wood 1½ x 1½in (38 x 38mm), which are glued and nailed together at the corners. Bear in mind that the screen needs to be larger than the design you are going to print. If you are planning to print fabric in the future, the screen should be longer than the width of the fabric you intend to use.

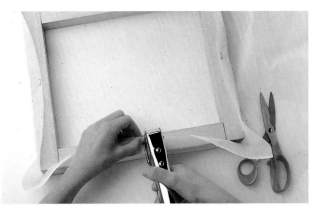

1 Butt join the ends, gluing and nailing them together using waterproof glue and 2in (5cm) nails or panel pins. Smooth the wooden edges with sandpaper and seal the frame with a coat of varnish.

2 Cut fabric 2in (5cm) wider all round than the frame. Screen fabric, which is available from screen printing suppliers, is ideal. Alternatively, use silk, nylon or cotton organdie. Stretch the fabric across the screen and staple or tack it to the sides of the screen, starting with the centre points of each side. Try to keep the weave of the fabric parallel to the sides of the screen.

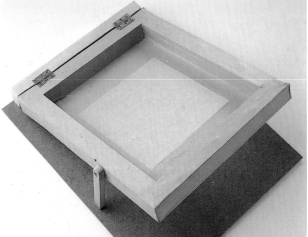

3 Mask the edges of the screen with tape on the underside and inside edges to cover a minimum of 1in (2.5cm) along the sides and 2in (5cm) at the ends. The tape prevents seeping and also provides 'reservoirs' for the dye.

To make a squeegee

Cut a length of doorstop rubber slightly shorter than the width of your frame. Sandwich this between two slats of planed wood, ¾ x 1in (19 x 25mm), cut to the same length as the rubber strip and screw together. Finally, stick a bar handle — a strip of planed wood 1 x 2in (25 x 50mm) — along the top of the squeegee. To enable you to rest the squeegee on the frame when not in use, the bar handle should be slightly longer than the width of the frame.

4 For the baseboard, choose a sheet of chipboard, plywood or blockboard — this can be either the same size as the screen or slightly larger. Nail a strip of wood 1½ x 1½in (38 x 38mm) along the width at one end. Place the screen fabric side down on top of the baseboard, butted up against the wooden strip you have just nailed in place.

Make a hinged joint so that the screen can be opened and lowered on to the baseboard. Use detachable butt hinges and fix them in position by opening them up, placing one side on the strip and the other on the screen, and screwing them down. A wooden support, which is screwed to the side of the frame to hold it firmly in an open position, is an optional — but useful — addition.

◁ There is no limit to the number of colours that can be used in one print. Here a total of five colours have been effectively combined.

▽ Screen printing can be used to decorate many different surfaces and materials — even bathroom tiles. Just use the appropriate inks.

◁ The charm of screen printing is that you can design your own fabric lengths. It is a perfect way to make very individual clothes, like this dramatic shirt.

◁ In addition to textiles for clothing, screen printing is an ideal way to create co-ordinated home furnishings — from curtains, to bedlinen and even rugs. This powerful design was used to decorate a mat.

Beginning screen printing

*A screen print can have several colours or just
one. For each colour you'll need a stencil, which is stuck
to the fabric mesh of the frame. To print, the dyes
are forced through the mesh and the stencil by pulling
the squeegee across the screen.*

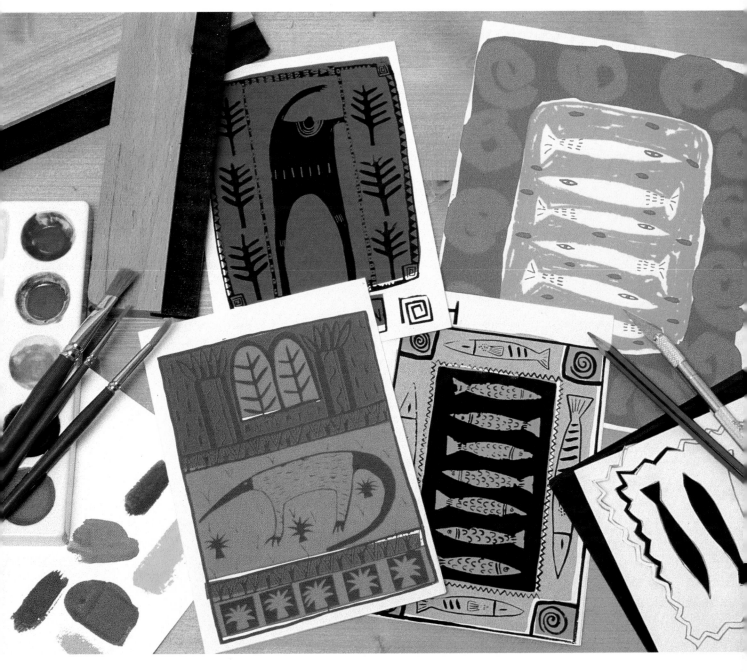

Once you have a screen and squeegee you are ready to start planning some designs. The attraction of screen printing is that even the simplest patterns and motifs can look wonderfully decorative.

Before embarking on any major projects, it's worth playing around with your chosen design to see what effects you can create.

It's best to use no more than two or three colours to begin with. Try out different colour combinations using crayons or shapes cut out of coloured paper. And experiment with various coloured and textured papers to see how they set off the colours you have chosen.

54

Materials and equipment

As well as coloured pencils or crayons, drawing and tracing paper, and a utility knife, you will need:

Printing colours

Colours for screen printing are available from arts and crafts shops. If you can choose oil-based screen printing inks, the screen will have to be cleaned with turpentine or mineral spirits. Craft and cold water fabric dyes (which must be mixed with a proprietary thickener) can also be used. Dyes for printing on paper can be used too, if they are waterproof.

Making a paper stencil

1 Sketch out your design, keeping the shapes fairly simple. Work on a sheet of paper that is the same size as the back of your screen so that the design can be drawn to the actual size.

2 Use coloured pencils or crayons to try out different colour combinations. To begin with it is a good idea to restrict your design to two or three colours.

3 You will get a much better idea of the finished result if you cut out the design in coloured paper shapes and arrange these according to the original picture.

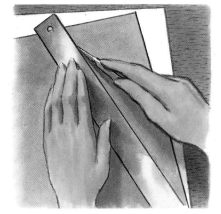

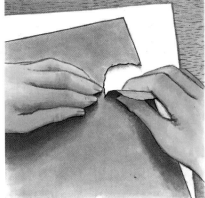

4 Your design will be more interesting if some of the shapes have straight, cut edges and others have ragged, torn edges. Use a utility knife or craft knife and metal ruler for the straight edges.

5 Random, jagged shapes are easily made by tearing the paper by hand. The torn edge reproduces exactly when printed and is a simple way of making the overall design look more unusual and effective.

6 Make a separate paper stencil for each shape. All the stencils must be the same size as the back of your screen. To make registration easier and ensure a successful result, trace each stencil from your original design.

Stencils

Paper stencils are the simplest to make. Special stencil paper is the most durable, but greaseproof paper also stands up well to continued use. For just a few prints you can use parcel paper.

For a long-lasting stencil use Pro-film, a transparent film with a peelable backing that allows you to cut away areas and leave the backing intact. You can also paint directly on to the screen with wax or shellac varnish to make a resist stencil. These will be discussed in more detail in a later section.

Paper

Any type of paper is suitable for screen printing, so choose one of a quality, texture and colour that best suits your design. The technique can also be used successfully on many other surfaces, including wood, plastic, metal, fabric and ceramics.

◆ TIP	DRYING PRINTS

A lot of surface space is needed for laying out wet prints. A good alternative is to make an indoor line with a length of string and hang each print by a corner with a plastic clothes peg.

Printing paper stencils

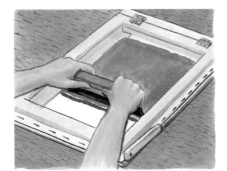

1 Mark the corners of the first stencil on the screen with pencil so that each next stencil can be positioned correctly. Fix the first stencil in place with masking tape.

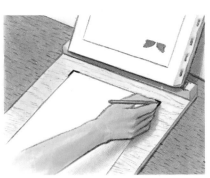

2 Place the first sheet of paper on the baseboard, marking the position of the corners. This will enable you to place all further sheets in the correct position for printing more sheets of the same colour and for printing the subsequent colours.

3 Mix all the colours needed for the print, ensuring that there are no streaks or lumps. The ink should be the consistency of thick cream. Pour a line of colour along the masked edge on the inside of the screen, keeping this away from the cut-out stencil shape.

4 Tilt the squeegee towards you and pull it firmly across the screen, ensuring that the ink covers the whole motif. Repeat the process by pushing the colour in the opposite direction, back to the other end of the screen.

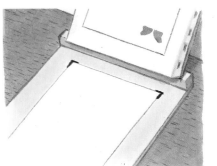

5 Lift the screen, remove the paper and hang up to dry. Place another sheet of paper in position and repeat the procedure for desired number of prints.

Wipe away excess ink and wash the squeegee. Remove and discard the stencil, and wash the screen with water (use mineral spirits or turpentine for oil-based inks). Allow the screen to dry.

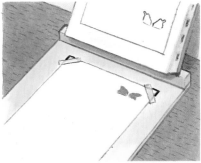

6 Fix the second stencil to the back of the screen, using the registration marks on the screen to position the stencil accurately. Put each sheet back on the baseboard, using the registration marks on the board. Repeat the printing and cleaning process for this and any further colours.

Butterfly print

Start with a simple motif in one or two colours. If you decide to print a two-colour design, make sure that each colour is easy to register. This motif is an ideal beginner's project because it won't affect the final design if the gap between the wings of the butterfly varies slightly.

You will need
◇ A screen
◇ Small quantity of two dyes
◇ Squeegee
◇ Stencil knife
◇ Stencil paper or parcel paper
◇ Tracing paper
◇ Quality paper for printing and matching envelopes if desired
◇ Cutting board or surface
◇ Pencil
◇ Masking tape

Preparing the stencil

1 Trim two sheets of stencil paper so that they are both slightly smaller than the base of the screen. Keep the corners square to make registration easier.

2 Design the stationery by tracing the motif in position on a spare piece of the stationery paper. This will be your master design for cutting the stencil.

3 Centre your design on the stencil paper. Mark outer edge and trace the motifs.

4 Lay the second piece of stencil paper on top of the first and trace the paper outline and motifs a second time. Be as exact as possible so that the stencil will be in registration.

5 To make the first stencil, lay the traced stencil on the cutting surface and using the stencil knife, cut out the top wings of the butterfly and the antennae.

6 Repeat for the second stencil, this time cutting out the two bottom wings of the motif. Make sure that the design is registered before you cut out the motif.

Printing the design
Print the design as described on the preceeding page.

△   The butterfly motif is the size used for the stationery. Try printing it in either one colour or different colours.

TIP	DESIGN IDEAS

There are two ways of preparing a stencil. In this project the motif is cut out of the stencil and it prints as a solid shape, with the background unprinted.
It is possible to reverse this and print the background, leaving the motif as the negative shape, or unprinted. To do this, cut out a shape or motif from stencil paper. Prepare your printing surface and dyes. Using the masking tape, mask off the area on the back of the screen that is to be printed in solid colour. Position the motif on to the surface to be printed, then carefully place the screen on top of this. Follow the printing process.

Screen printing techniques

*Screen printing enables you to apply a
variety of designs to fabric to produce your own decorative
fabric lengths. It is an ideal way to transform
ready-made items or inexpensive lengths of plain cotton into
bright and cheerful original creations.*

Designs suitable for screen printing can be adapted from many different sources, such as a wallpaper border or a favourite picture. An existing pattern in a room can be adapted to make co-ordinating accessories — the designs for our duvet cover were inspired by the fish border. Use these motifs or be inspired by your furnishings.

Materials and equipment

A screen, at least 6in (15cm) larger all round than the largest design to be printed. (For details on screens, see page 51.)

Self-adhesive vinyl This is cut into shapes to make the stencil. When the ink is applied to the screen it passes through the open cut-outs in the stencil to the fabric beneath. For differently sized stencils, vary the scale of a design by enlarging or reducing it, using a photocopy machine or graph paper.

Craft knife and **cutting mat** for cutting stencils.

Ink Use water-based textile inks. Choose either transparent or opaque inks, depending on the effect you wish to achieve. For permanent designs on washable fabrics the ink can be heat-set following the manufacturer's directions.

Squeegee This needs to be ½in (1.2cm) narrower than the inside measurement of the frame.

Fabric Use pure cotton fabric which has been prewashed, cut to the desired size and pressed. Alternatively, use a plain white duvet cover.

You will also need **plastic sheets** to protect your work surface, **paper** and a **towel** to raise the printing surface and **paper tissues** to clean the stencil.

Preparing the design

1 Use your own adapted designs or copy and enlarge the motifs shown in this section.

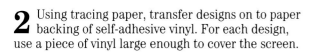

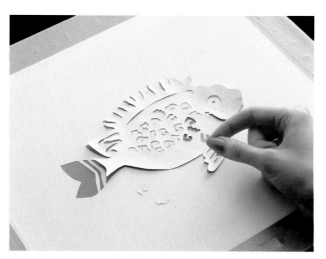

2 Using tracing paper, transfer designs on to paper backing of self-adhesive vinyl. For each design, use a piece of vinyl large enough to cover the screen.

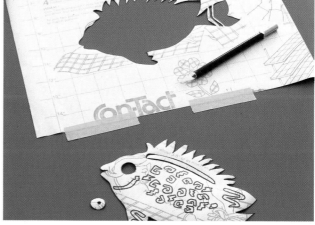

3 Tape self-adhesive vinyl to cutting board and, using the craft knife, cut along the traced lines on the self-adhesive vinyl.

4 Carefully remove the paper backing from the first stencil to be printed. Apply this side of the vinyl to the underside of the screen, making sure that it completely overlaps the duct tape border — to prevent any seepage of ink. Apply any cut-out details, such as the scales, gills and the eye.

5 Turn the screen over and press down firmly on the mesh, taking care to secure all the cut edges of the stencil to the screen. Tape along the outside edges of the vinyl, taking the tape up on to the frame. This prevents unwanted ink seeping on to the fabric during printing.

Printing on to fabric

1 Place the plastic sheet over the work area, making sure you cover the table and floor as well. Have a clothesline ready to hang the painted fabric on to dry between each printed image.

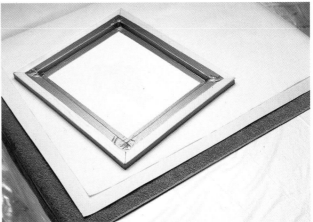

2 Place a towel over plastic sheet on table — the padded surface helps make a better print. Cover towel with a sheet of paper. Place fabric, right side up, on top of paper; if printing a duvet cover, put cardboard between the layers of material to prevent paint seeping through. Put screen on top of fabric.

3 Place 2-3tbsp of ink along the vinyl next to the design area or along the border. Applying firm, even pressure, use the squeegee to pull the ink back and forth across the screen until the ink is evenly distributed over the stencil area.

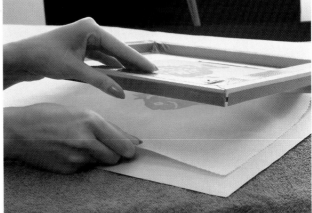

4 Lift the screen slowly, taking care that the ink does not run on to the fabric; carefully peel off the fabric. Between prints, rest screen so one edge is slightly elevated; rest squeegee on a stand or lid. Hang screen-printed fabric on clothesline to dry.

5 As soon as you have finished using the first stencil remove it from the screen. Using a soft cloth, wash the screen and then leave it to dry thoroughly. Wash the stencil and, if desired, affix it to waxed paper for

reuse on another piece of fabric. The screen is now ready for the second and any subsequent stencils. Follow the previous steps for preparing and printing each design.

Trouble-shooting problems

To prevent problems occurring, it is a good idea to practise your screen printing techniques on a spare piece of the material to be printed before beginning to print your chosen item. For example, too many pulls of the squeegee across the screen causes the ink to soak through the fabric and bleed, while too few causes the print to look patchy or incomplete.

Patchy or incomplete print

If the print looks uneven or blotchy, this is because the screen has become clogged with excess ink. This happens when the ink is too thick and has had time to dry on the screen between prints. To prevent this happening on subsequent prints, thin the ink to a better consistency, following manufacturer's directions and gently wipe the clogged screen with a soft tissue.

Uneven patches of colour

If areas of the print appear bare and the ink has not been properly transferred to the fabric, this is because the ink has been unevenly applied or the squeegee has not been pulled across the screen often enough. To prevent this from happening again, make sure you are using the correct amount of ink and pull the squeegee across the screen a few more times.

Ink soaks into fabric

If the colour of the printed image looks very dense and has bled into the surrounding fabric, blurring the edges of the design, too much ink has been used or the squeegee has been pulled across the screen too many times. On subsequent prints, use less ink and take care not to overdo it with the squeegee.

Ink runs at design edges

If the edges of the print look blurred, either the ink is too thin or the edges of the stencil have not been pressed firmly to the screen. This is remedied either by mixing the ink to a thicker consistency or ensuring the edges of the stencil are pressed down flush to the surface of the screen.

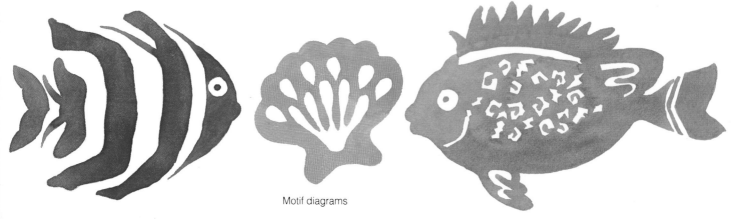

Motif diagrams

Lino printing

*Lino printing — another method of block
printing — is a quick but effective way of decorating anything
from paper, such as giftwrap, to fabric items, such
as napkins. A design is cut into the lino, which can then be
printed out using brightly coloured inks.*

Lino printing is a relatively modern method of printing, dating from the early 1900s. The basic technique is similar to that of block printing. The printing blocks are made of linoleum, on which a design is drawn and gouged out using sharp cutters. It is then called a lino cut.

Design ideas

Decorate a sheet of paper to make giftwrap paper and make a matching greetings card, or design your own invitations for a special occasion such as a birthday, Christmas, or for a wedding.

Choose a simple design of your own to begin with, or trace off a picture. Alternatively, you could use traditional symbols, such as wedding bells, birthday cakes, Christmas crackers and snowmen, or even names as simple motifs. Templates for embroidery or stencilling can also help to provide inspiration for designs.

You can also transform everyday things, such as plain notepaper and envelopes, handkerchiefs or napkins, into original and individual objects, with a lino print pattern. A pretty design around the border, or a small motif in each corner, can quickly and effectively provide an attractive finishing touch. It is, however, easier to master the technique by working on paper or posterboard, than on fabric.

Planning a design

Make sure that you keep your design simple, since complicated details cannot be cut into lino. Most designs rely on fairly large, basic shapes, with few intricate lines. The best effects are often achieved by using the motif sparingly in a small area, and as a repeat pattern for a larger area.

Once you have chosen your design, decide which areas of the pattern you wish to show printed *before* you start cutting Remember that the uncut parts of the lino will show the printed image, while the cut areas will remain unmarked.

Colour schemes

When choosing colour schemes, a combination of a light colour on a darker background often works well. Alternatively, try using effective contrasting colours, such as black on white, or purple on yellow. A mixture of two vibrant colours, such as crimson red and turquoise, also works well.

Tools and equipment

Newspaper is used to cover and protect the work surface.
Tracing and carbon paper and a pencil are used to copy the design on to the lino block.
Lino is available from craft shops and comes in different sizes. It should be quite thick.
Cutters It is a good idea to buy one handle and a variety of cutting blades, which will slot into the handle. Alternatively, buy each cutter as a separate tool. The cutters must be sharp and, therefore, easy to use. Use your tools with care and always follow the instructions carefully.

Three blades are enough to obtain a varied pattern: use a wide gouge to remove large areas, a small V-cutter for fine lines and a large V-cutter for wider lines. A sharp knife may also be useful.
Ink Use either oil-based or water-based printing ink. Since water-based ink is easy to clean up, it is more suitable for children to use.
A ceramic tile is used to roll the paint out on thinly and evenly .
Masking tape is useful for holding the board or paper in place.
Ink roller is needed to transfer the ink on to the lino cut.

Posterboard or paper to print on.
Rolling pin This is firmly rolled over the back of the lino to transfer the design from the block to the card or paper.

Cutting lino

Lino hardens at low temperatures, which can make cutting difficult in cold weather. Make it more pliable by placing on top of a radiator or in a very low oven for a few minutes every half hour. Alternatively, place it between two pieces of brown paper and lightly iron it whenever it becomes difficult to work with.

The cutting is done with simple cutters and gougers. Always cut away from your body, making sure you keep both hands away from the cutting edge. Begin by cutting shallow trenches round the areas to be gouged out. Holding the cutting tool in the palm of your hand, push it into the lino, smoothly following the lines of your design. (For more intricate work use a sharp knife.)

Use the wider cutters to gouge inwards from the groove to remove large areas. This technique helps to avoid accidentally cutting into the relief area of the design. Remember that lino cuts cannot be repaired once they have been cut into.

TIP	MOUNTING LINO

Lino is usually bought unmounted. But, if it is going to be used repeatedly, mount it on a wooden block (use plywood or soft wood), about $\frac{1}{2}$in (1.2cm) thick, using wood glue. This will make it last longer and it will be easier to handle. To print the design, hit the block with a wooden mallet.

Giftwrap and card

Either copy the butterfly template, or use a design of your own. To make the wrapping paper, use it as a repeat pattern over the entire sheet. Use a single butterfly motif for the greetings card.

You will need
◇ Newspaper
◇ Tracing paper
◇ Carbon paper
◇ Pencil
◇ Lino block
◇ Tool handle and cutters
◇ Lino printing roller
◇ Rolling pin
◇ Ceramic tile
◇ Lino ink (in colours of your choice)
◇ Coloured paper or card to print on
◇ Masking tape

Cutting the lino block

1 Completely cover your work surface with newspaper. Using a pencil, draw the design on tracing paper, making sure that it is the right size to fit on the lino block.

2 Position the carbon paper between the tracing paper and the lino block and secure in place with masking tape. Retrace the lines of your design to transfer it to the lino. Remove the paper, taking care not to smudge the image.

3 Use a small V-shaped cutter to cut along the pencilled outlines of your design and a wider V-gouger to cut larger areas. Cut curves by turning the block, keeping the cutting tool firmly in your hand.

4 When you have finished cutting the design out, wash the lino cut in warm water to remove any loose fragments of lino. Leave it to dry thoroughly before starting to print.

Printing

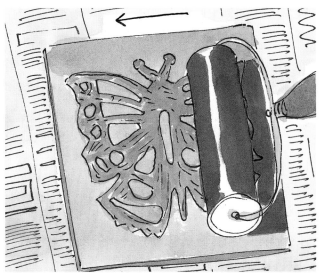

1 Squeeze some lino ink (in the colour of your choice) on to a ceramic tile. Push the roller over the ink until the roller is thinly and evenly coated with a layer of ink.

2 Run the inked roller over the lino cut until all the raised areas are evenly covered with ink. Make sure you apply the paint very sparingly, or bubbles may form which will spoil the texture of the printed pattern. Use a cloth to carefully remove any excess ink from the grooves.

3 Using masking tape, secure the corners of the coloured paper (to be printed on) to the work surface. Place the lino cut, inked side down, on the paper. Then firmly run a rolling pin over the back of the lino to transfer the design to the paper. Lift up the lino carefully.

4 Repeat this printing technique until you have as many patterns as you desire. (You do not need to repaint the lino for every single print.) Make sure that you do not print the separate motifs too close to one another; if they overlap, they will blur and spoil the finished design.

5 When you have finished, wash the tools and the lino cut in warm soapy water.

Marbling basics

*Marbling is a highly decorative technique used
to embellish paper, fabric and three-dimensional objects. The
simplest technique involves decorating paper and
the finished designs can be used as wrapping paper or to transform
boxes and other small items.*

The art of marbling is an ancient one which probably originated in Japan. The patterns are made by floating colours on a liquid and then transferring them to paper, fabric or small objects. It should not be confused with the more sophisticated paint effect of the same name, which uses paint brushes to simulate marble.

The technique is best suited to paper, however it is possible to marble small objects, such as candles or blown eggs. To marble fabric a more advanced method is used. This technique, which uses a Carragheen moss size, is explained in the next section.

Each marbled pattern is unique and cannot be duplicated. Once the floating colours have been lifted from the surface, the design cannot be repeated and new colours are used for the next piece of marbling.

Using oil and water

This is the simplest way to marble and is ideal for creating lively patterns in which accidental colour combinations and patterns contribute effectively to the end result.

The technique involves floating oil paint on water (that is preferably at room temperature). As oil and water don't mix, the colours remain on the surface of the water and are then simply lifted off.

The paint is normally dropped on to the surface using a pipette or artist's brush. However, you can create a bolder effect by pouring the paint on to the water.

When dropped into the water the paint, ideally it should be the thickness of cream. If it is too thick it will simply sink.

paint, ideally it should be the thickness of single cream. If it is too thick it will simply sink.

Once on the surface, the paint can be teased into a variety of random pattern effects by moving it around with a thin stick or blowing gently across the surface with a drinking straw. A wide-toothed marbling comb drawn over the surface gives a distinctive swirling effect.

Using size

For more detailed and defined marble patterns, the paint can be floated on to size (a very thin wallpaper paste) instead of water. Although the principle is the same, the thicker medium gives you more control over the finished effect as it prevents the paint from moving around so freely. Size should be used at room temperature.

Materials and equipment

Paint

Oil-based paints, such as artist's oil paints are ideal. They are available from most art shops and as they have to be thinned with a little mineral spirits before use, a little goes a long way.

Size

You can buy wallpaper or artist's size from specialist outlets. Alternatively, you can make your own gelatine size (see right).

Container

You can use any watertight container as long as it is large enough to take your chosen paper. Try using a large baking tin, developing tray or cat litter tray.

Paper

Marbling works well on all types of paper except those that are very thin or exceptionally thick. Typing paper is ideal and a manageable size. Brown parcel paper, cartridge papers, or one of the many tinted papers, available from artist's suppliers and good stationers, can also be used.

Tools

The only tools you will need are a palette or small jars for mixing paint, old paint brushes, and a thin stick, knitting needle or wide-toothed comb for pattern making (turn over the page for instructions on making a marbling comb).

◆ TIP	GELATINE SIZE

To make gelatine size, dissolve a tablespoonful of gelatine powder in 1pt (450ml) of hot water. Thin with another 1pt (450ml) of cold water and allow to cool. The mixture should resemble a thin liquid, rather than jelly.

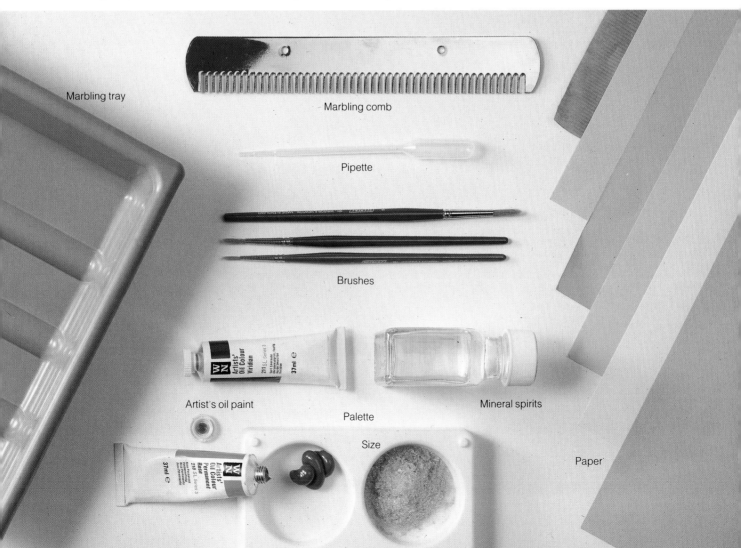

Marbling tray

Marbling comb

Pipette

Brushes

Artist's oil paint

Palette

Mineral spirits

Size

Paper

Marbling paper

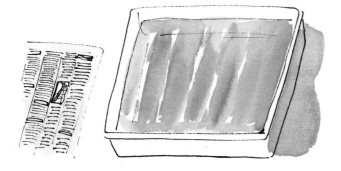

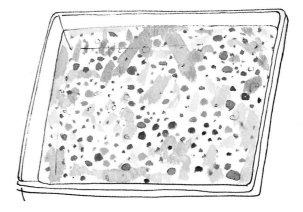

1 Half fill a container with water (or size) and place several sheets of newspaper close to it, ready to receive the wet marbled sheet. Squeeze a little artist's oil colour into a palette or small jar and mix with mineral spirits. The colour should be the approximate consistency of cream.

2 Drop spots of colour on to the water. The colour will spread out to form discs on the surface; the thinner the colour, the further it will spread. If the colour sinks to the bottom, it is too thick. Repeat with subsequent colours taking care not to overdo it; two or three colours are sufficient.

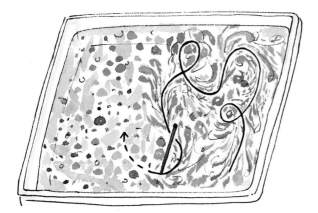

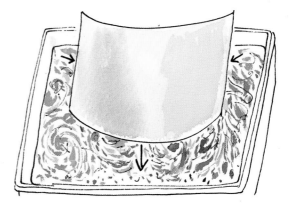

3 With a stick or knitting needle, blend and manipulate the colours. Alternatively, pull a wide-toothed comb across the surface to break up the colour into a distinctive feathered pattern.

4 When you have a pattern which pleases you, lower a sheet of paper on to the surface. To avoid air bubbles (which leave blank areas on the paper), hold the paper at either end and allow the curved centre of the sheet to touch the water first. Carefully lift out the paper and place on newspaper.

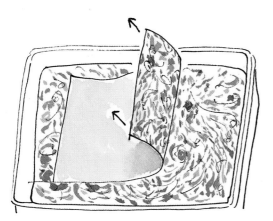

5 You will find that some paint remains on the surface of the water and you can often take a second or even a third print from this. Just tease the colours a little to blend them. Alternatively, remove the residue of colour by drawing a strip of newspaper across the surface before starting again.

6 The marbled paper will be dry enough to move after about half an hour. However, do not handle it too much as oil colour takes a long time to dry thoroughly (leave for at least a day). To flatten the finished work, weight it by covering it with plain paper and placing it between the pages of a large book.

Making a marbling comb

You can make a marbling comb from thin posterboard, pins or needles and glue. Make several combs with different tooth spacing.

 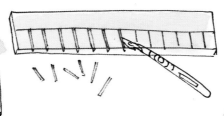 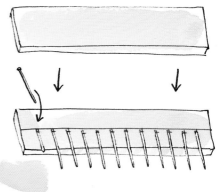

1 Cut two 2in (5cm) wide strips of posterboard to a length slightly shorter than your marbling tray. Draw a line, lengthways, down the centre of one of the strips. On one half, measure and mark out the position of the teeth.

2 With a sharp utility knife, cut shallow grooves from the centre line to the edge of the posterboard – do not cut completely through the card.

3 Press the needles into the slits so that the sharp ends protrude by at least 1in (2.5cm). Firmly glue the second strip of posterboard on top of the first, enclosing the needles. Finally, seal with varnish or white glue.

Decorative desk set

For this beautiful desk set, you can re-cover items that you already have or you can make your own from cardboard. Blue, green and red were used for the marbling shown here.

To make your own desk set, choose stiff posterboard and use a metal ruler and a sharp craft knife for cutting. Corners and joins should be stuck with a suitable strong adhesive.

You will need
◇ Marbled paper
◇ Adhesive (not water-based)
◇ Craft knife
◇ Metal ruler
◇ Desk set

To make the desk set
Marble the paper according to the instructions on the previous page and leave until thoroughly dry. Cut the marbled paper to cover the pencil holder, letter case and blotter, allowing enough margin all around for seams and corner folds. Stick the marbled paper firmly in position with adhesive.

Marbling techniques

*Many beautiful and intricate marbled patterns,
such as those found on the covers and endpapers of books or
on expensive looking scarves and handkerchiefs,
can be made by floating colours on a special size made from
Irish seaweed, or Carragheen moss.*

Seaweed marbling

Unlike simple water and oil marbling, seaweed marbling provides you with absolute control over the pattern and colours. This enables you to create intricate designs on the surface of the size which can then be transferred intact, without losing any of their detail or precision. This method not only enables you to marble on paper, but also on pieces of fabric.

Materials and equipment
Paint

You can buy specially prepared water-based marbling paints. They are generally the consistency of cream, however, occasionally the colours thicken and need to be diluted. When this happens, add a very small quantity of water.

Carragheen moss

This is a specialist seaweed available dried from health stores, or in powder form from art and craft shops. For marbling, the seaweed should be powdered, so dried Carragheen moss must first be ground in a coffee grinder.

Moss size preservative

Moss size preservative should be added if you intend to keep the size solution for more than 24 hours. Once the preservative has been added, the size can be put in a jar and saved for further use.

Oxgall

Oxgall is used to dilute the specially prepared marbling colours and is available from craft shops and specialist marbling suppliers. It should be used sparingly and drops should be measured with a pipette or eye dropper. The amount required depends to some extent on room temperature — the colder it is, the more oxgall you require.

Alum

This is a colourless, soluble substance used for treating paper and fabric before marbling. Alum brings out the strength and brightness of the colours and makes them more permanent. It also makes the surface more absorbent and receptive to the colour.

Fabrics

Choose thin cotton or silk fabrics, preferably in pale shades or white. Dark fabrics can be used, but the marbled colours will be affected by the deeper base colour. All fabrics must first be washed to remove any 'finish' or dressing. This makes the material more receptive to marbling colour.

Marbling comb

Specialist combs are available. However, an Afro comb, or an ordinary comb with some teeth removed, is a good substitute. You can also make your own following the steps in the previous section.

Preparing to marble
Mixing size

To make Carragheen moss size, mix a tablespoon of powdered Carragheen moss with 2pt (1 litre) of cold water in a large saucepan. To prevent the mixture going lumpy, mix the powder with a little of the water, then gradually add the rest. Slowly bring to the boil, stirring continuously. Boil for 5-10 minutes, stirring all the time.

Dilute the mixture with 2pt (1 litre) of cold water and strain through a piece of muslin or old tights to remove any lumps. Pour the size into a large baking tin or other shallow container and leave for at least 12 hours before using. The finished mixture should be the consistency of runny jelly.

If you intend to keep the size for more than a day or so, add a few drops of moss size preservative to the cold size before it sets.

Using oxgall

To help the colour spread easily over the surface of the size, a small amount of oxgall is added to each colour. Put a dessertspoon of paint in a small jar and add four drops of oxgall. Mix thoroughly.

Using alum

Before you can begin to marble your chosen paper or fabric it must first be treated with a solution of

alum. This makes the surface more receptive to the colour and helps 'fix' it. To make an alum solution, dissolve two tablespoons of alum crystals in 2pt (1 litre) of hot water. Allow to cool.

To treat paper sponge the solution over the side to be marbled. Place the treated sheets under a heavy book or board to keep them flat and use while still damp.

To treat fabric soak each piece in the solution for about 20 minutes. Allow to dry, then press with an iron. Use within one week.

Testing colours

Before you begin it is is a good idea to try out different colour consistencies on the size.

Drop a spot of colour on to the surface; the colour should spread easily. If it does not spread out or it sinks, you need to add a little more oxgall. If the colour still doesn't spread, it may mean that the size is too cold. The size should be at room temperature, so try adding a little warm water. If your test colour spreads very rapidly and thinly, it probably contains too much oxgall, so add a little more paint.

When you are satisfied with the consistency of all the colours you are using, clear the surface of the size by carefully skimming it with a strip of newspaper.

Making patterns

Patterns are made by dropping colours on to the surface of the size and arranging them to obtain the effects you want. As moss size retains every detail and colours stay clear and separate (no matter how intricate the design), the finished design will be as clear and detailed as the pattern you create. The technique is therefore ideal for making combed and sprinkled patterns.

To make a dense pattern, with little or no surface base showing, use a lot of colour. For a lighter effect, scatter small amounts of the colour sparsely over the surface of the size.

Combing

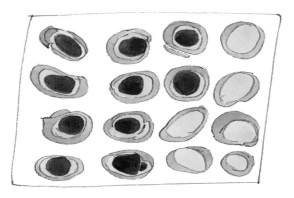

1 Apply the first colour in spots across the surface of the size, allowing 4in (10cm) between each spot. Place a drop of the second colour into the centre of each expanded spot. Add further colours in the same way. The second colour will need a little more oxgall than the first, the third more than the second, and so on.

2 To join the spots into feathery stripes, pull the colour across the width of the tray using the tip of a paint brush handle. Work in alternating directions across the tray, until the colours form a regular pattern.

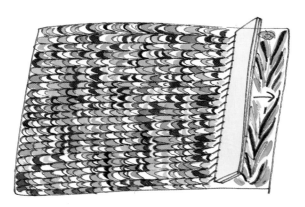

3 Finally, with a marbling comb, drag the stripes down the length of the tray keeping the teeth of the comb just below the surface of the size. The pattern is now ready to be transferred to paper (using the technique shown in the previous chapter) or to fabric (as shown on the following page).

Sprinkling

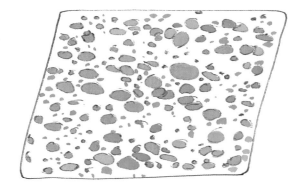

1 Apply the first colour so that the expanded drops of paint almost cover the surface of the size. It is not necessary for the drops to be regular or evenly spaced.

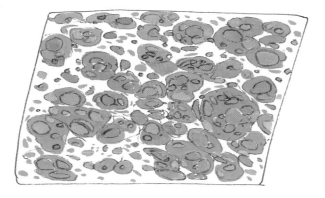

2 Drop the second and subsequent colours on to the first. The second colour will need a little more oxgall than the first, and the third needs more than the second.

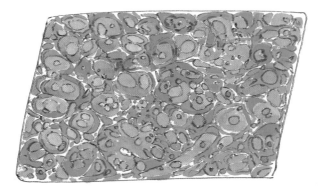

3 The final colour should retain the shape it is dropped in, while the previous colours are pushed together to form sinuous strands across the whole of the pattern area.

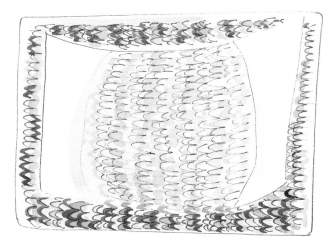

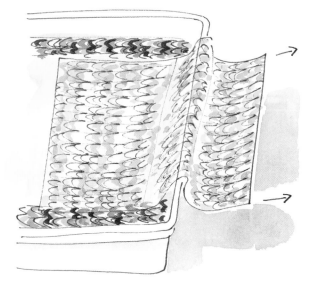

1 Lay the alum-treated fabric on the patterned size by holding it at each end and lowering it gently in to the tray until it rests on the bottom. Lower the fabric centre first to avoid air bubbles being trapped between the fabric and the paint.

2 To remove the marbled fabric, pull it gently to the edge of the tray. Keep as much of the fabric in contact with the base as possible as you slide it out. Rinse under running water to remove excess colour, wring and allow to dry naturally. If the colour runs excessively, increase the amount of alum when preparing fabric.

Marbled scarf

These beautiful marbled head-scarves are made by following the instructions shown above.

You will need
◇ Scarf or square of silk or fine cotton
◇ Marbling colours
◇ Carragheen moss size
◇ Moss size preservative (optional)
◇ Oxgall
◇ Alum
◇ Marbling tray (large enough for the scarf or fabric)
◇ Pipette or eye dropper
◇ Stick or comb for pattern-making

You will achieve better results if the marbling is carried out on a light background, so start with a white or pale fabric — the light tone will not affect the brightness of the colours you choose.

If you are using a piece of fabric it can be hemmed either before or after marbling. Alternatively, buy plain or pale-coloured ready-made scarves in cotton or silk. Remember to wash the fabric to remove any dressing, and remove any labels.

Pleated lampshades

These elegant lampshades have been made using sheets of pleated, marbled paper.

When making your lampshades it is important to take into account the position of the finished lamp and the surrounding colour scheme. Pale colours are translucent and give off a lot of light. Darker colours, being more opaque, will block out the light. In this case, the effect is altogether more dramatic and the lampshades will produce sharply contrasting areas of shadow and pools of light. Choice of paper is also important, as it must hold crisp folds. Try a test piece before cutting out the shade. Strong drawing paper is ideal. Remember to use low wattage bulbs with paper shades.

You will need
◇ White lampshade frames or rings
◇ Button thread, needle
◇ Marbled paper
◇ Grosgrain ribbon
◇ Ruler and sharp pencil
◇ Adjustable leather punch
◇ Tape measure or string

1 Measure the circumference of the base ring using a tape measure or piece of string and cut the paper to twice this length. If you are using a frame, the depth of the paper will be 1½in (4cm) more than the height of the strut of the frame. This allows the shade to extend ¾in (2cm) top and bottom.

If you have to join the sheets of paper, allow an extra inch (2.5cm) overlap allowance at each end.

2 Lay the paper face downwards on a smooth surface. With the ruler and pencil, mark parallel lines 1¼in (3cm) wide across the width of the paper. At the same time, mark guidelines for the holes ¾in (2cm) from each long edge.

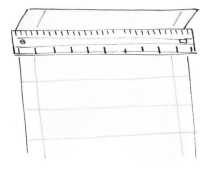

3 Lay the edge of the ruler along the first mark and fold the paper over it to make a clean crisp line. Repeat to make folds all along the strip.

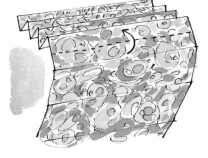

4 Turn the paper over, and match the first fold line to the second. Press to form a crisp concertina fold. Repeat until the whole strip is folded into concertina pleats.

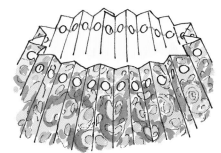

5 Use a leather hole punch to make holes centrally through both layers of each pleat, following the guidelines. Use a small setting for the bottom holes, and the largest setting for the top ribbon holes. Curve the shade round, overlapping the first and last pleats; trim overlap if necessary. necessary.

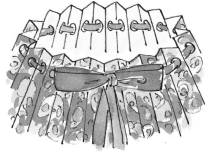

6 Run the ribbon through the top row of holes, draw together to fit the ring and tie in a decorative bow. Run button thread through the bottom row of holes, pull to fit the bottom ring of the shade and tie to hold in place.

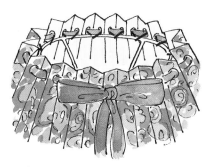

7 Slip the shade over the frame or top ring. Use a needle and button thread to lace the shade on to the ring, threading through a pair of holes, over the ring, and back through the next holes. Tie the ends of the thread, then repeat for the second ring.

PATTERN LIBRARY

Sprinkling

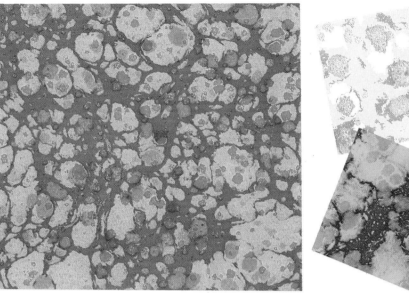

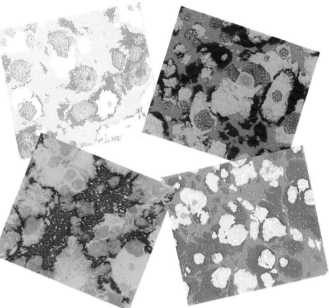

Combing

Swirling

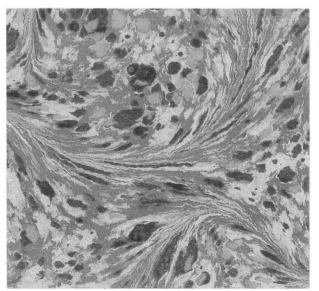

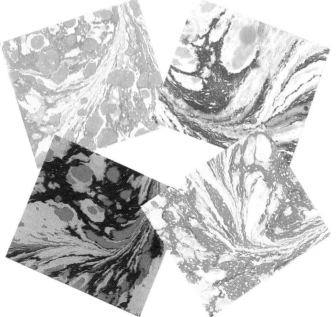

PAINTING ON FABRIC

Painting on fabric

*These colourful geometric designs were done with
a pot of yellow fabric paint and a permanent black felt tip pen on
plain cotton. By designing and colouring your own
fabrics, you can create unique accessories and furnishings without
being restricted to mass-produced materials.*

Applying colour to fabric

There are a various techniques for painting fabric. Some, such as Chinese brush painting and batik, need special materials and a little practice, while others, such as the methods shown here, are extremely simple and enable the complete beginner to create artistic and pleasing results.

Materials and equipment

As well as having the usual design tools, such as a craft knife, ruler, cardboard and paper on hand, you will also need to invest in specialist paints and pens.

Paints

Unlike fabric dyes, paints do not penetrate the fabric. The colour is painted on to the surface of the material and does not sink in. However, it is possible to thicken certain dyes to make them suitable for painting. Most paints are applied with a brush, but certain types come in tubes and these can be drawn or dribbled directly on to the fabric straight from the tube.

You can buy opaque, transparent or pearlized paints in a wide range of colours. Most brands are ready prepared and require no mixing. Some brands need to be thinned slightly. Once completed, the design is fixed in place with an iron or steam, according to the manufacturer's instructions.

Fabric pens

Special fabric pens come in a range of colours, and are available with fine or broad tips, (like felt tip pens). They are easy to apply and are fixed to the fabric by ironing.

Fabric pens are available from chain stores, hardware shops and craft outlets. They are ideal for outlines, geometric patterns and writing on fabric.

Choosing fabrics

It is important that the fabric and paints you are using are compatible. On the whole natural fabrics are the best choice. Some paints can be used on a variety of fabrics but you will find that results differ depending on the composition and thickness of the fabric. The same colour and brand of paint may look entirely different when applied to silk and cotton.

The truest colours are obtained by painting on to white fabric. When painting on dark fabrics you will probably need to use an opaque paint, otherwise the fabric colour will show through and affect the final result. Opaque colours are readily available, but if you cannot find the right opaque colour, transparent colours can be made opaque by adding some white fabric paint. When using a pale colour on dark fabric, some manufacturers recommend painting the design in white, then applying the intended colour on top.

Before starting to paint your design, you should wash your fabrics to remove any 'dressing'.

Creating designs

Be imaginative and creative when planning your design and choosing colours. We opted for bold, geometric shapes when painting the cushion covers and tablecloth featured here, but your own designs should reflect your taste and individuality.

The most important thing is to avoid fussy, overcomplicated designs. Start with simple shapes and patterns and limit yourself to a few colours. Your ideas can be spontaneous, involving the minimum amount of planning, or you may prefer a more considered design. For inspiration, look through books and magazines and at colours and designs already in the room. Try taking ideas from Nature — leaf shapes, flowers, shells and fish are all rich sources of design ideas. Alternatively, experiment with geometric shapes such as squares, triangles, rectangles and circles.

When you have decided on your theme, sketch a few selected shapes on to stiff card, keeping these simple and bold. Cut out the shapes and try arranging these in various ways on a sheet of paper until you are pleased with the result (the card shapes are then used as templates for drawing round when you transfer your design on to the item being decorated). If you are still unsure about the finished effect, it is a good idea to try out your ideas first on some fabric.

▷ *Although these brightly coloured cushions look very different, they have, in fact, all been created using the same basic templates. Clever arrangement and design lends each one its own geometric individuality.*

Geometric cushions

White cotton cushion covers have been decorated in bold shapes of black and yellow. However, this simple geometric design is extremely versatile, and works equally well on table napkins and other items of household linen.

You will need

◇ White cotton cushion cover, napkin or other fabric item
◇ Black fabric pen
◇ Black and yellow fabric paint
◇ 2 artists' brushes
◇ Posterboard for templates
◇ Craft knife and cutting board
◇ Metal or plastic ruler
◇ Embroidery marker pen
◇ Plastic sheeting or newspapers (to protect surface)
◇ Spare fabric (to test colours)
◇ Pencil, felt pen and paper

1 Wash and iron the item to be painted (even newly bought articles should be washed thoroughly to get rid of the 'dressing' on the fabric). If you are working on a cushion cover or pillowcase, place a sheet of plastic or board inside to prevent any colour seeping through.

2 Start by cutting two templates from stiff cardboard. The design here is based on two squares measuring 10in (25cm) square and 3in (7.5cm) square, but you may prefer a bolder or more scattered effect, in which case the templates should be larger or smaller.

3 Cut a sheet of paper to the same shape as your fabric and arrange the templates on the paper in a design you like. Draw around the shapes in pencil. Your design will be more interesting if your shapes overlap and are occasionally taken over the edge of the paper.

4 When you have a design that pleases you, decide which parts of the overlapping shapes are to be 'on top'. Draw over your pencil lines with felt pen, ignoring the areas to be overlapped.

5 Transfer the design on to the fabric, using your templates. Draw directly on to the fabric with the fabric pen or draw out the design with an embroidery marker before tracing over it with the pen.

6 With the fabric pen, start filling in the shapes with dots, stripes or zig zag patterns. You can divide some of the shapes into grids, using a ruler, or draw circular shapes and curved lines. Colour in selected areas using black or yellow paint.

7 To fix the colour, follow the manufacturers' instructions. This is usually done by covering the design with a clean piece of cloth and ironing over it.

TIP	USING A MARKER

A water-soluble, embroidery marker pen is a useful aid to designing. You can draw out your pattern on the cloth and remove any parts you don't want by dabbing the outline with a damp cloth. When the fabric is washed, any pen marks will be removed.

PATTERN LIBRARY

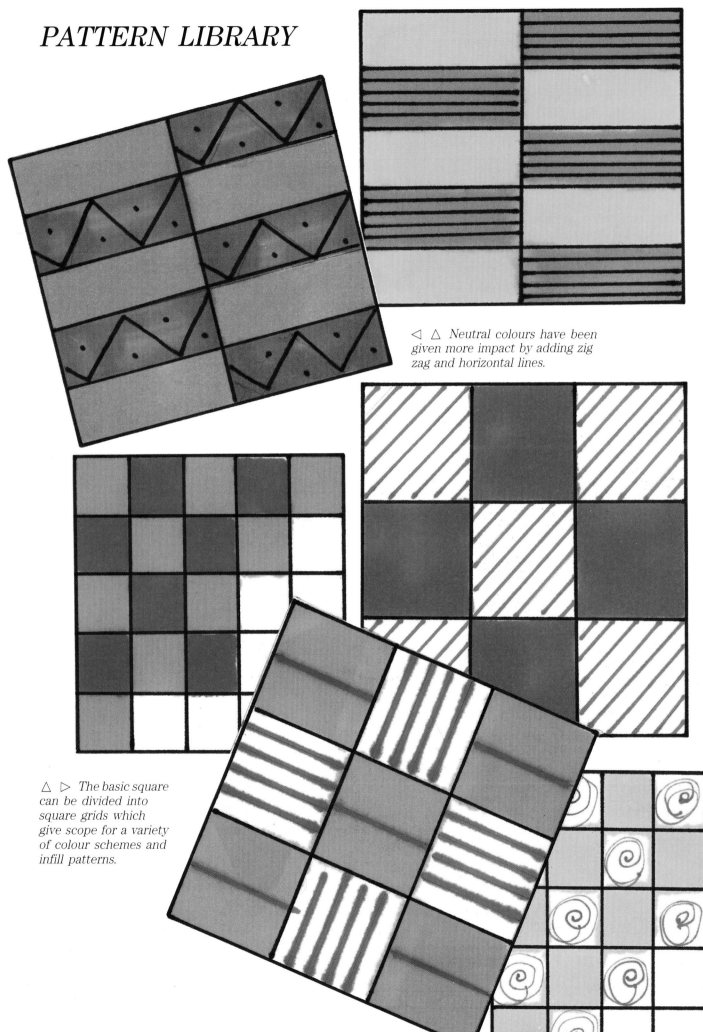

◁ △ *Neutral colours have been given more impact by adding zig zag and horizontal lines.*

△ ▷ *The basic square can be divided into square grids which give scope for a variety of colour schemes and infill patterns.*

Painting on clothing

*Rethink your wardrobe this summer, and step
out in a riot of pattern and colour. With the easy-to-use fabric
paints now available, it takes just minutes to turn
everyday clothing — shirts, jeans, skirts, shorts and shoes — into
brilliant and unique fashion garments.*

Why pay the earth for a hand-painted fashion item, when you could create your own for a fraction of the cost? The idea may seem a little daunting at first, but if you start off with a T-shirt or scarf and follow a few simple rules, you will soon master the technique.

Materials and equipment

Apart from a domestic iron for fixing the colours, you will need the following materials:

Colour mediums

There are now several brands of fabric paints on the market, available in a range of colours including gold, silver and a few fluorescent colours. The paints in art and craft shops may be water-based or may need to be thinned with a proprietary diluter, ask your dealer.

For greater control when drawing fine lines and outlines, try fabric pens. They look like felt tips but have been formulated for use on fabric. They are not suitable for painting large flat areas.

Also available are 'heat-expanding' colours, paints that puff up and stand out from the surface of the fabric. It is also possible to buy 'expanding' medium, which can be mixed with regular fabric paints to obtain the same three-dimensional effect. These are especially popular with youngsters for T-shirt designs.

Colours are generally fixed by pressing with a domestic iron on both sides of the fabric.

Fabrics

Fabric paints can be used with all types of fabric, whether synthetic or natural.

On heavy and non-absorbent fabrics the colours do not diffuse, and the brushstrokes will retain their shape. Use the colours undiluted. The addition of a thickening agent makes direct painting easier. Initially the thickener will make the fabric stiff, but the stiffness will disappear in the wash.

With finer fabrics, you might find the paint easier to apply if it is mixed with a little painting medium which softens the colours without increasing fluidity. Ask your dealer for the appropriate product.

On very fine, soft fabrics, such as silk, colours tend to spread anyway and it can be difficult to get a sharply defined shape. For free-hand painting, this is fine, and the soft shapes and blobs of colour can often be successfully incorporated into the design. Alternatively, you can 'outline' the shapes with gutta, a transparent fluid, available from art and craft shops. When the gutta outlines are completely dry, they act as barriers to prevent the colours from seeping into the adjoining areas.

Brushes

For painting freehand shapes, artists' brushes are best. The type of brush you use affects the mark you make (see right), so it is worth experimenting. Fabric paints are water soluble and brushes should be washed immediately after use.

Painting clothing

New garments should be washed to remove dressing. This will help the

△ *A plain white jacket is personalised by the imaginative and careful use of fabric paint.*

colour take to the fabric and withstand further washing.

Fabric for painting should be taut, so stretch the garment on to the work surface and fix with thumbtacks before starting work.

With jeans, shirts, shorts and other items which involve a double thickness of fabric, slip a protective layer of paper or plastic between the two layers before starting to paint. This will stop the colour from seeping through and spoiling the underside of the garment. Wait until the colour is dry before moving the garment.

If you want to paint the back of the garment, wait until the first side is quite dry, turn the garment over, and repeat the process.

Painting freehand

Some of the prettiest patterns are those painted on to the fabric without any drawn outline and without using a ruler to make straight lines. If your confidence is not up to this 'freehand' approach, make a faint line drawing with tailors' chalk which can be washed out later. Alternatively, make a bold line drawing with a fabric pen, and retain the line as part of the design.

Flowers and leaves are ideal for freehand painting. You can either work from imagination, or you can find a suitable photograph or picture to use as a starting point. Try to make your own flower and leaf shapes simple and large, painting them with bold and sweeping strokes. Squiggles, wavy lines, and simple fish and bird motifs lend themselves to this direct painting approach.

Freehand shapes

Keep your design simple — some of the most effective marks are the easiest to make:

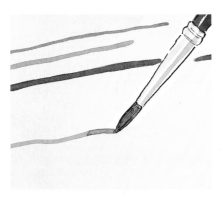

A thin line is painted by holding the brush upright and using the tip of the bristles.

A regular, broad line is made by applying even pressure to the brush.

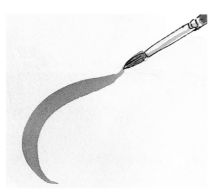

An undulating line is made by varying the pressure on the brush.

Small dots are done with the tip of the brush.

Larger, oval dots are made by pressing down with the bristles at a slight angle.

Simple flower petals can be made by pressing down with the side of the bristles.

Brushmarks

The mark you make depends to a large extent on the brush you use. Artists' brushes come in a range of sizes, and the bristles are shaped differently according to the purpose they serve:

Round

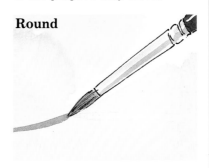

This is the most popular of all artists' brushes. The metal holder, or ferrule, holds the bristles in a narrow round shape, making it an ideal brush for painting thin lines and other delicate linear forms.

Flat

Here, the short, square-cut bristles are held in a flattened ferrule. The 'flat' is ideal for filling in areas of colour and for making thick, regular lines.

Filbert

Somewhere between the 'flat' and the 'round', the filbert is good for painting strong, tapering strokes, and for making undulating lines. It is ideal for thin, sinewy leaves and petals.

Painted canvas shoes

You will need:

◇ A pair of canvas or fabric shoes
◇ Red, blue and yellow fabric paints
◇ Black fabric pen
◇ Round artists' brush

You will find it easier to paint one colour at a time. In this case, the yellow dots were done first, leaving plenty of room between each one for other colours. Red and blue patterns were added, and the paint was allowed to dry. Finally, fabric pen was used to circle the yellow dots.

△ Painting on canvas shoes can be further enhanced by adding other decorative features. The flowers painted on these shoes have centres of pink and red beads.

△ Simple canvas shoes are made into fun fashion accessories by painting them in bold, colourful designs.

Quick and easy fabric paints

These easy-to-use fabric colours are perfect for painting simple, abstract designs on all items of clothing, including T-shirts, shoes and bags. The no-mess colour is squeezed directly from the tube on to the fabric, making it possible to create spontaneous designs.

△ *Small, abstract motifs made with expanding paints guarantee a good result — like these simple designs, drawn on to a sweater.*

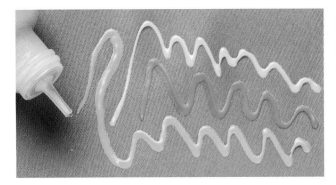

△ *Some expanding paints need to be set with an iron to make them puff up on the fabric. This sample shows what the paint looks like before heat is applied.*

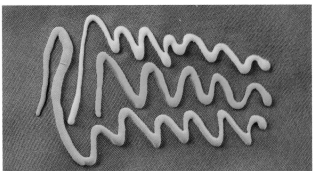

△ *When heat is applied to the wrong side, the paint puffs up from the surface taking on an entirely different character, as this sample shows.*

Expanding paints are applied straight from the tube to the surface of the fabric. They are called expanding paints because they literally swell or puff up on the surface of the fabric as they are squeezed from the tube, or when heat is applied to them. One of the pleasures of working with expanding paints is actually watching them grow and puff up.

The texture of the paint can vary — some brands give a matt, rubbery surface, others a hard shiny line.

This, coupled with the fact that the paints are available in a wide range of colours, means there is a lot of scope for creating inventive patterns.

Complicated designs are not necessary. In fact the paints can be tricky to handle as they take up more space in the design once they have expanded. This must be taken into account when planning the design to avoid the paints running into one another. Fine figurative designs are nearly impossible to produce unless you have access to screen printing facilities.

But don't be put off — expanding paints have a wonderful texture and the best results can be achieved by using them to make simple, geometric patterns. Just a row of dots can look effective, especially if the colour scheme is well thought out. Once the surface of the paint has puffed up, it will definitely stand out on any background - even black.

Materials and equipment

Apart from a domestic iron, used with certain brands of expanding paints, you will need a selection of colours available from art and craft shops and the fabric or item of clothing to be decorated.

Paints

Expanding paints are packaged in flexible bottles or tubes which have a nozzle attached so that the paint can be applied directly to the fabric. Some brands of paint swell on contact with heat and must be ironed from the reverse side of the fabric once they are dry. Other brands expand on contact with the air and swell as they leave the tube.

Fine line paints

Some expanding paints are specially made to imitate embroidery. They come in tubes with very fine nozzles and are used to produce patterns which look as if they have been worked in running stitch or cross stitch.

Fabrics

Expanding paints can be used successfully on most fabrics - even leather and suede. However, the paints do not work well on very fine or sheer fabrics like chiffon, as once dry, the paints are quite heavy and the fabric will not support them. Also the rubbery texture of the paint does not suit the feminine quality of these

◁ *Dots and circles of expanding paint, give this pullover an original look. The pastel colour scheme is appealing against the beige knitted background.*

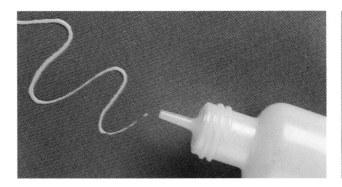

△ *Some brands of paint expand on contact with the air as the paint comes out of the tube. This one creates a fine line which is useful for small design details.*

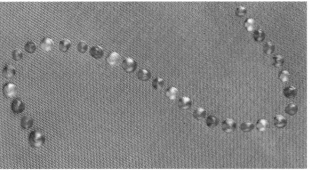

△ *Some expanding paints have a rubbery, matt texture; others, like the dots above, have a sleek shiny surface. Try combining two textures in one design.*

delicate fabrics. Clothing that has been decorated with expanding paints should be hand washed; machine washing may cause the paint to crack or crumble.

Colour schemes

Let the garment and its background colour dictate the colours you are going to use. A feminine, pastel top would suit a dainty motif, in soft tones, while a bright sweatshirt would call for a bold pattern in strong colours. Test the look of the colours on a hidden part of the garment or scrap of fabric before you start.

Creating a design

Expanding paints, especially those that are set by an iron, puff up a lot, so take this into account when planning a design. Steer away from intricate, finely detailed patterns, as the paint will be difficult to control and the pattern may be lost if the paints expand more than you expect. Practise working with the paints before you settle on a design, so that you can see how they handle and what they look like when they have been set. The key to creating a strong design in expanding paints is colour choice, so put as much effort into colour selection as you do designing the actual motifs.

Random, geometric patterns guarantee a good result — so start with polka-dots, dashes, squiggles and zigzag lines. Abstract floral motifs can also work well. Lettering is effective, but best results will be gained if the letters are marked out in dots rather than straight lines.

Using expanding paints

Preparation

The surface of the garment or fabric should be completely flat. For best results stretch the garment or fabric out on an old piece of wood or heavy cardboard. Secure it in place with thumbtacks.

Planning

Plan the design before you start. For a simple pattern you may want to work directly on to the fabric. Transfer a more complicated design on to the fabric with dressmaker's carbon paper or chalk. The design colour could also be drawn on lightly in pencil.

Painting

Outlines and fine lines can be drawn straight from the tube; draw these in first. You can make thicker lines by applying more pressure. Use a paint brush to fill in any large areas.

Fixing the paint

Fix the paint according to the manufacturer's instructions. You may need to iron the reverse side of the fabric with a domestic iron. This is done when the paint has dried.

▽ *This whimsical design suits the texture of expanding paints. The largest areas in the design can be filled in with a paint brush.*

Dotted jersey

A plain chocolate brown jersey is transformed using expanding paints. The pattern is simple — just rows of dots, but the subtle colour choice makes it effective.

You will need
◇ A plain jersey in a strong neutral colour
◇ Expanding paints in white, plus four strong pastel colours
◇ Thumbtacks
◇ A work surface, eg heavy cardboard

Painting the design

1 Lay the jersey out flat on an old work surface and secure it with thumbtacks.

2 Apply dots of white paint directly from the tube, spacing them evenly all over the garment.

3 Start from some of the white dots and make rows of dots using the different pastel colours. Vary the direction and combination of the colours.

4 Allow the paint to dry, then fix it according to the manufacturer's instructions. Turn the jumper over and repeat the process until the entire surface is patterned.

▽ *The rubbery texture of these expanding paints contrasts well with the smooth yarn used to knit the jumper. Random dots, applied all over the surface of the knit, are simple do and look striking.*

Textured fabric paint

*Experiment with various fabric paints, colours
and techniques to create stunning and original textured effects
on silk. There is no need to restrict this
technique to decorating white fabric — textured paint effects
also work well on coloured fabrics.*

Use the various types of fabric paint to create a lively range of different textures and interesting effects. For example, use fabric pens to highlight finer details, and glitter paints and expanding paints to add texture to a design. All the designs shown here are fairly abstract; the 'watercolour' painting technique has been used to create the background designs. This can be embellished with fabric pens, glitter paints and expanding paints.

For more information about painting on silk, see pages 115-118 and 127-132.

Preparing the silk

Follow a few simple steps to prepare the fabric before painting. Note that coloured silks may distort the colour of fabric paints and pens, so use strongly contrasting colours, or paints which sit on the fabric, such as glitter paints.

1 Wash the silk to remove the manufacturer's finish. Leave to dry completely, then press.

2 Stretch the silk over a frame before starting to paint. Secure one side of the fabric along one edge of the frame with silk pins. Then stretch the fabric across the frame to the other edge, keeping the tension even, and secure in the same way.

Choosing fabric paints

Many types of textured fabric paints are readily available from craft shops and stationery stores. A range of different textured effects can be achieved using silk paints, glitter paints, expanding paints and fabric paints, pens and crayons. More than one type of paint can be used on the same piece of fabric to create interesting designs with a variety of textures. When fixing the paints always follow the manufacturer's instructions for each type you have used as methods can vary.

For more information on using fabric paints, pens and crayons, expanding paints and silk paints see pages 77-88, 93-96 and 115-118.

Glitter paints

Glitter paints are made from a glue-like substance in which glitter is suspended. They are produced by various manufacturers and can be applied directly from the tube or with a brush. When the glue dries, only the glitter remains visible. As the glitter remains on the surface, this paint is suitable for both light and dark fabrics.

Using coloured silk

Before painting a piece of coloured silk, it is important to experiment to find out how the colour of the fabric affects the appearance of the paint. For example, light-coloured and transparent paints do not show up on very dark fabrics. With strongly coloured silks, use a paint that is darker than the fabric. Alternatively, use either expanding paint or glitter paint — this sits on the surface of the fabric rather than sinking into it.

The criss-cross and spiral designs below have been painted on to a piece of green-blue silk.

Criss-cross design

This bright and cheerful design, below left, combines silk paints, fabric pens and glitter paints.

1 Using silk paints, paint blue crosses and green lines. Leave plenty of space around the lines and crosses as silk paints spread slightly. Leave to dry.

2 When the paint is dry, outline the crosses with a fine-nibbed fabric pen. Then use a thick-nibbed fabric pen to give a hard edge to the lines.

3 Using green glitter paint, make green glitter crosses as shown. Then add a central dot of blue glitter paint to the blue crosses.

Spiral pattern

The psychedelic design below was created by brushing diluted yellow silk paint over the coloured fabric to produce abstract patches of vibrant green. Expanding paint was used to form a raised spiral pattern.

1 Dilute equal amounts of yellow silk paint with water; sponge randomly on to silk. Leave to dry.

2 Draw fine spirals using white expanding paint. Leave to dry; iron the reverse side of fabric to fix and puff up the paint.

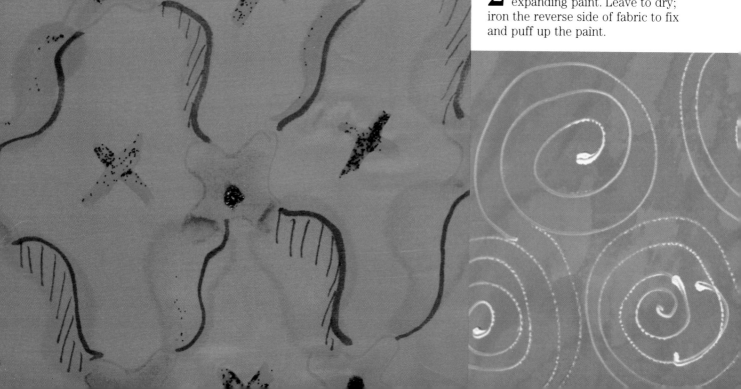

Rainbow effect

This is a wonderful example of the watercolour silk painting technique. Loose bands of colour were painted on to the surface in gentle zigzags and allowed to bleed into one another freely to create a dazzling spectrum of colours. Glitter paint was used to add texture.

1 Using a dropper, paint large sweeping zigzag patterns in yellow, red and blue silk paints. The colours will blend together to create purple, green and orange, shown above. Leave to dry completely.

2 To finish, add dashes of gold, red and blue glitter paint.

Blue and green dream

In this design the naturally textured surface of raw silk gives extra texture to the overall pattern. The steps are shown from left to right, with the final sample below.

1 Mix equal amounts of turquoise silk paint and water; paint over the entire surface of the silk. Add drops of undiluted green silk paint, allowing room for the paint to spread. Leave to dry.

2 Add drops of undiluted turquoise silk paint between the green patches. Leave to dry.

3 Add big smudges of green glitter paint over the green patches to highlight them and to add extra texture.

4 Finally, add small dots of gold glitter paints randomly over the surface of the silk.

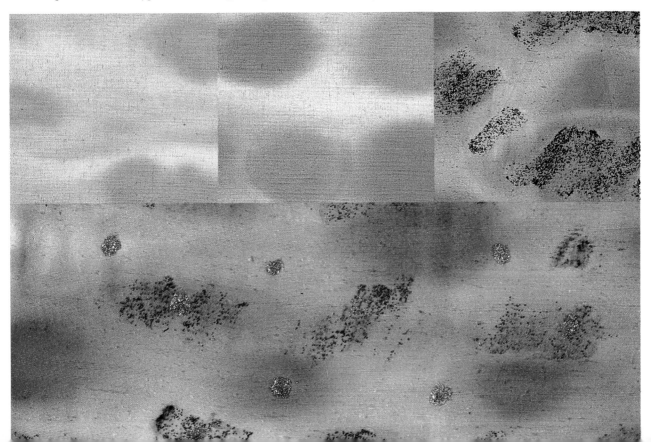

DESIGN LIBRARY

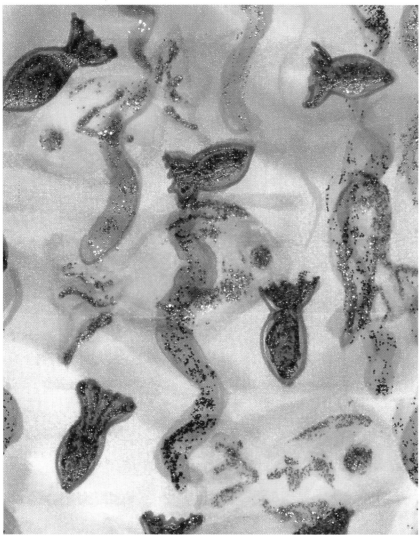

Use fabric pens to add definition to shapes, (centre right and bottom right); use glitter paints to highlight selected areas, (above, top right and bottom centre) and use puff paints to add texture (bottom left).

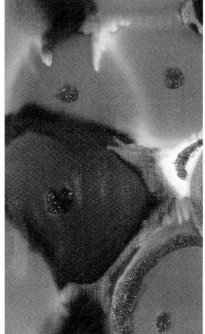

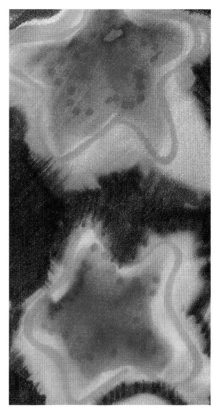

Fabric pens and paints

*Coloured fabric pens and paints can be used
to make bright patterns on ready-made accessories and
clothing. A simple design painted in bold primary
colours, such as yellow, blue and red, can look stunning painted
on a T-shirt, or used as a repeat pattern for a hem.*

Fabric pens and paints are not only great fun and easy to work with, but can enable you to add a personal touch to plain, everyday items of clothing. For the best results, choose simple designs and bright primary colours. Look through children's col-ouring books for design inspiration; or you could even try copying a child's drawing!

Children love working with brightly coloured paints and pens too; so give the whole family the op-portunity to let their imagination run riot. The end results can be made into all kinds of useful items, from T-shirts to duffle bags; you could even make a matching set of bed linen. The fabrics you create can also be used in other crafts, such as patch-work or appliqué.

Materials and equipment

For more information, see the fabric painting sections.

Fabrics

For bright and colourful results, choose cotton. It is also a good idea to experiment on various fabrics before starting to paint.

Preparing fabric Always wash and iron fabrics before painting. This allows for any shrinkage and also removes any artificial finishes which would prevent the material from absorbing the paint properly.

Fabric pens and paints

Fabric pens work well on most fabrics, although the colours bleed slightly on sheer fabrics and may not show up on very dark material.

Use fabric pens on their own, or with fabric paints, to highlight or outline areas, and to add scribbles, doodles and dots to a design. Do not use them over large areas as the overall effect might be patchy.

Fabric paints are available in a wide range of colours and can be used on most fabrics, but check the manufacturer's instructions first Be careful when mixing or diluting colours, as too much water will cause the colour to streak or smudge. The drying process for paints can be speeded up with a hairdryer; but do not expose the fabric to direct sunlight, which will fade and spoil the colours.

Fixing colour Fabric pens and paints are fixed by ironing at a high temperature. Once fixed, the colours are fully machine washable and fade resistant.

Brushes

An ordinary, cheap paint brush is satisfactory for applying the paint, although a good quality sable brush is easier to use and gives better results. Since fabric paints are water soluble, brushes should be thoroughly rinsed in warm water after use, and dried with a clean cloth. Careful rinsing is vital: any residue of paint left in the brush will clog the fibres and mark your fabric. Never leave a brush standing in water as it will be ruined.

A place to work

Choose a well-lit area, but away from direct sunlight. Use a large plastic sheet, an old cloth or old newspapers to cover the work table.

T-shirt

For best results keep the design simple. Either trace the tiger pattern on the template, or make up your own design. The size of the design should be about 8 x 8in (20 x 20cm). Keep the colours simple too; bright primary colours will work best.

You will need

◇ A child's white cotton T-shirt
◇ Black, thick-nibbed fabric pen
◇ Fabric paints in blue, green, yellow and red
◇ Piece of thick cardboard, large enough to fit inside the T-shirt
◇ Paper and pen
◇ Clothes pins

1 Trace the tiger design from the template on to paper, using a black pencil.

2 Position a piece of thick cardboard inside the T-shirt, so that the paint will not come through to the back.

3 Place the paper design between the cardboard and the T-shirt, so that the design can be seen through the material. Make sure the design is centrally positioned and straight. (You could secure it by taping the paper to the cardboard.) Keep the T-shirt tightly stretched by clipping the material at each corner with clothes pins.

4 Trace the design on to the T-shirt, using the fabric pen. Make sure that the material is kept taut while tracing, so that the design is visible through the fabric. Be careful not to make mistakes — these pens are permanent, even before the colours have been properly fixed.

Actual size trace diagram

5 Once the design is traced on to the material, remove the paper template, but do not remove the cardboard. The T-shirt is now ready to paint. The paint should not be too runny, or it will bleed and spread — test it on a scrap of the same fabric first.

6 Once you have finished painting the design, leave the paint to dry completely. Finally, remove the cardboard.

7 To fix the colours, cover the T-shirt with a clean, dry cloth, then iron on a very hot setting for a couple of minutes. Wash the T-shirt before wearing.

An animal border

The hem of the delightful skirt pictured on the opening page has been decorated with fabric pens to produce a merry circus of animals. The design was drawn on to the fabric before it was made into a skirt.

You will need

◇ Piece of material, large enough to make a child's skirt: we used 52in (132cm) of 45in (115cm) wide polycotton fabric
◇ Thick cardboard
◇ Fabric pens in black, yellow, blue and red
◇ Paper and pen
◇ Clothes pins

1 Trace the animal border template on to a sheet of paper. Place the paper design between the fabric and a piece of thick cardboard — you must be able to see the design

through the material. Secure in place with clothes pins.

2 Using the black fabric pen, copy the outline of the design on to the material. You need to repeat the design across the width of the material, making sure that there are no obvious joins between each pattern repeat. In order to make a full skirt, we painted two borders across the fabric width.

△ *Transform a plain T-shirt with bright fabric paints or pens.*

3 When you have finished copying the outline, you can begin to colour in the other areas. It is easiest to use one colour at a time, using the template as a colour reference. Be careful not to smudge the colours.

4 Fix the colours in the same way as for the fabric paints.

◆ **TIP**   **AVOIDING ACCIDENTS**

Always remember that fabric paints will stain cloth permanently, even before they are properly fixed, so wear an apron to protect your clothing and cover your work area with newspapers or an old cloth. Paints are easily knocked over by accident, so keep them on a tray to avoid creating too much mess.

◆ **TIP**   **STORING PAINT**

Paints are very sensitive to direct heat and bright lights, both of which can spoil the colour and consistency of the paint. Therefore, make sure the lids on the paint jars are tightly closed after use. Then store them in a cool place away from direct light and, as a safety precaution, out of children's reach.

Actual size trace diagram

Transfer painting

*Transfer paints and crayons allow you to paint
and draw a design on paper before ironing it on to fabric; a
practical idea for artists who lack confidence.
Use as many colours and textures as you want in the design; the
details will transfer like magic on to fabric.*

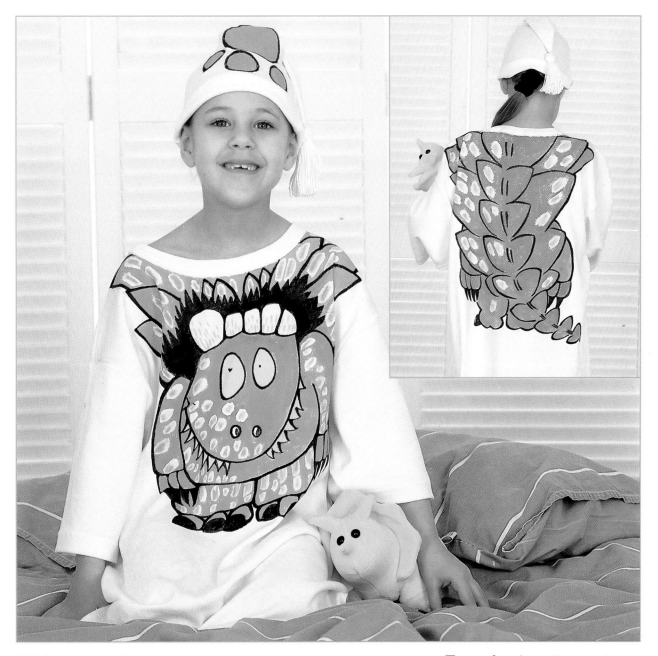

Making transfers

The great advantage of working with transfer paints and crayons is that the colours and patterns can be worked out on paper and then transferred on to fabric. Changes or mistakes can be corrected, or you can start again, without ruining the fabric to be decorated.

Unlike ordinary fabric paints and crayons, which are applied directly to the material, transfer products look as if they have been printed rather than painted and drawn.

Transferring the design

Designs are transferred by placing the paper face down on the fabric and then pressing the back for a few minutes with a medium hot iron. It is important to follow the manufacturer's instructions but, generally, the hotter the iron the brighter the colours. A design can be used twice but the second image will be paler than the first.

Reverse transfers

It is important to remember that the design will appear in reverse when transferred on to the fabric. With abstract patterns and flowers this does not matter too much. However, if there are any letters or numbers in the pattern it is vital to get it right. In this case, it is easier to draw the design the right way round on tracing paper; you can then apply the paint or crayons to the reverse side by following the lines of the drawing which are visible through the transparent paper.

Materials and equipment

Apart from a few general items such as **an iron, a pencil, paper** and **paint brushes,** you will also need a selection of **special transfer paints, crayons** or **pencils** in colours of your choice.

Transfer paints

Available in small jars from art and craft shops, transfer paints come in a limited range of colours but can be mixed to make other colours. In the jars they look very dark and dull, but when transferred to the right fabric they are bright and vivid. The type of fabric decorated dictates the strength of the final colour: it is therefore important to test each colour before using it.

Transfer paints are at their best when used for small areas of

Using transfer paints

△ *Simple shapes are perfect for practising transfer techniques.*

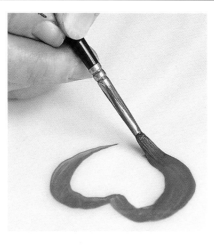

1 Use an artists' brush to paint the colour on to a sheet of paper. You can use tracing paper or any other type of paper as long as it is sturdy enough to withstand the heat of the iron.

2 Cotton swabs are useful for removing thick paint and for making pale areas such as the shine on this apple.

Doily patterns

Doilies make pretty patterns that are especially effective as motifs on bed linen and tablecloths.

1 Use a whole doily or make up your own pattern by cutting out separate motifs as shown here.

2 Paint the right side of the doily and then arrange the pieces face down on the fabric. Cover with a sheet of paper and press according to the manufacturer's instructions.

3 Lift each piece carefully one at a time, checking that the colour is strong enough before removing them.

colour, such as spots and stripes: they can also be dripped or spattered on to the fabric. It is more difficult to transfer a large area of flat colour because the heat has to be applied evenly and it is difficult to avoid making marks with the iron.

Transfer crayons

Transfer crayons look similar to children's blackboard chalks: they have a crumbly textured effect which can be transferred exactly on to fabric. You can make different colours by scribbling one crayon over another. They are transferred in the same way as the paints.

Transfer pencils

A transfer pencil looks exactly like an ordinary drawing pencil, but with one useful difference — it works in the same way as transfer paints and crayons. Use it to draw on paper and then iron the drawing on to fabric. The pencils are often used for transferring embroidery designs on to fabric, as the lines are very fine and are easy to disguise with embroidery stitches.

Suitable fabrics

Transfer paints and crayons work best on synthetic fabrics. On nylon, polyester and other synthetic materials, the colours are extremely bright. If you use mixed fibre fabrics, such as cotton-polyester, the colours tend to come out as pastel shades. On cotton, wool and other natural fibres, the colours are usually very pale.

3 Allow the paint to dry, then carefully position design face down on fabric and cover with a thick sheet of paper or newspaper.

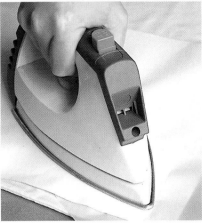

4 Hold the iron firmly over the motif, moving it around to avoid burning the paper. See the manufacturer's instructions for the length of time required and the correct iron temperature.

5 Carefully lift a corner of the transfer sheet without changing its position. If the colours are too pale, replace the transfer and apply a little more heat. If the colours are satisfactory, remove the paper altogether.

△ *Doilies make interesting designs.*

▽ *This pretty pastel design is ideal for toddlers' clothing.*

Using transfer crayons

1 Start by drawing your design on paper. If you are using letters and numbers, such as this ABC design, remember to do the design in reverse.

2 The transfer method is the same as for paints. Position the design, chalk side down, on the fabric and cover with a sheet of paper. Move the heated iron around slowly on the paper for a few minutes, then lift one corner to

check that the colours are strong enough. If not, replace the transfer sheet and apply the heat for a little longer.

3 When the colours have been transferred to your satisfaction, peel back the transfer sheet and remove it.

Dinosaur nightshirt

You will need
◇ White polyester T-shirt
◇ Green transfer paint and pink transfer crayon
◇ Black permanent marker
◇ Two large sheets of drawing paper ·
◇ A pantograph (available from most art shops)
◇ Black fabric pen or laundry marker

1 Using the pantograph and the drawing paper, enlarge the photographs of both the back and front of the dinosaur, making sure the back and front drawings join up at the shoulders.

2 Paint the green areas with transfer paint, leaving small, irregular white patches for the pink spots. Fill in the centre of each white patch with pink transfer chalk.

3 Position the paper, painted side down, on the T-shirt and apply the heated iron. Move the iron around to make sure the entire design is properly transferred. Then remove the transfer.

4 Slip several sheets of newspaper inside the shirt so that the ink does not seep through, then draw round the outline, nose, eyes and other features with a chunky fabric pen or laundry marker. The black lines will look better if you allow the thickness of the line to vary slightly.

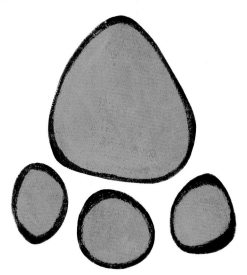

Matching nightcap

The nightcap, made from fabric to match the nightshirt, is decorated with a cotton tassel and paw print.

You will need
◇ White fabric, cut into two triangles each with a base of 9½in (24.5cm) and sides of 16½in (42cm)
◇ Needle and cotton
◇ White crochet cotton
◇ Red and white transfer paints

1 Start by making up the nightcap: with right sides together, sew down the two longer sides of the fabric triangles, taking a ½in (1.2cm) seam allowance. Hem the open end.

2 Make the tassel by cutting 6in (15cm) lengths of white crochet cotton. Group them together, then fold in half and secure with cotton, tied 1in (2.5cm) from the folds. Attach the tassel to the pointed end of the nightcap.

3 Draw, paint and heat-fix the paw print design as for the dinosaur nightshirt.

Animal print fabrics

Go on safari with bright and striking animal print clothing. These designs, inspired by the amazing markings of wild animals, such as cheetahs, zebras, tigers and giraffes, prove that you do not have to use elaborate patterns and colour schemes to create successful fabrics.

The coats of many safari animals are striped or speckled in rich colours for camouflage. For centuries people have sought to acquire these animals' sleek and elegant appearance by using their skins to make clothing.

You can now capture the beauty of animals in a far more friendly fashion by copying their markings and colourings on to material, using fabric pens and paints. This enables you to make stylish, yet inexpensive, fashion garments and accessories for both adults and children. You do not need to go on safari or to a zoo to see wild animals; look at natural history books for inspiration.

All you need for the animal prints are a selection of fabric paints and pens and some material — cotton works best, but you could experiment with textured fabrics, such as velvet.

Tiger print

To accurately and successfully re-produce the stripy tiger look, you must blend and shade the back-ground colour before adding the stripes. The top of a tiger's back is a rich, reddish brown colour which gradually becomes lighter, until it reaches a creamy colour on its belly.

You will need
◇ Cotton fabric — pre-washed to remove manufacturer's finish
◇ Fabric paints: we used brown, black, red, yellow and white
◇ Black fabric pen

Method

1 Stretch the material over a piece of cardboard and hold in place with clothes pins. This makes the surface easier to work and, when painting a ready-made item of clothing, prevents paint seeping through to the back.

2 Mix the fabric paints to make a creamy white colour. If necessary, dilute with water.

3 Starting at the bottom of the piece of fabric, begin to paint the background using the creamy white colour; as you work upwards, darken the paint mixture by adding some brown and red. Add more colour at the top for the rich reddish brown of a tiger's back.

4 Leave the background colour to dry completely before adding the stripy tiger markings. Referring to the photograph of the tiger for design inspiration, make the outline of the vertical tiger stripes using a black fabric pen or black laundry marker pen.

Giraffe print

A giraffe's markings are ideal for painting on fabric. Each giraffe is totally individual in appearance: we have painted two pieces of fabric to reflect this — the top piece has very clear markings, while the shapes and colour of the bottom piece are less defined and blend together more.

You will need
◇ Cotton fabric — pre-washed to remove manufacturer's finish
◇ Fabric paints: white, brown, red and yellow

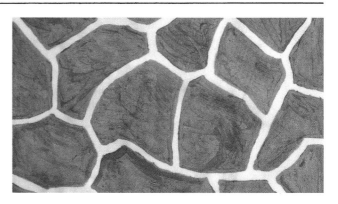

1 For design inspiration use the picture of the giraffe shown here. Prepare the fabric as given in step 1 of the tiger print.

2 Either leave the background white, or mix a creamy colour and paint on to the fabric. Leave to dry. Mix a rich russet brown colour and paint on large irregular patches of colour.

3 Leave to dry completely; fix the paints according to the manufacturer's instructions.

5 Fill in stripes with black fabric paint. Once dry, fix paint according to manufacturer's instructions.

Zebra print

Transform plain items of clothing and accessories with a striking black and white zebra design. Black and white stripes are always popular; by varying the shape and pattern of the stripes you can convert an average top into one that is far more dynamic and fashionable.

You will need
◇ Cotton fabric — pre-washed to remove manufacturer's finish
◇ Black fabric pen
◇ Black fabric paint

Method
1 Prepare the fabric or item of clothing as given in step 1 of the tiger print.

2 Referring to photograph and using black fabric pen, mark in lines for stripy zebra print. (If necessary, mark them in first using dressmaker's chalk.)

3 Fill in stripy lines with black fabric paint. Leave to dry; fix.

Cheetah print

For a realistic-looking cheetah print you should subtly shade the background colour of the fabric before adding the spotted markings. The shading is achieved by mixing two or three different earthy shades, including a creamy beige, a pale yellow and a darker tan; these are painted on to the background in random stripes. The cheetah's spotty markings are then painted with black or dark brown fabric paint. There is no need to confine animal prints to items of clothing — they look just as good on matching accessories, such as these sneakers.

Patterned sneakers

You will need
◇ A pair of sneakers
◇ Fabric paints: brown, black, red, yellow and white
◇ Black fabric pen (optional)

Method

1 Using fabric paints, mix a pale yellow colour; using this, paint vertical stripes at intervals around each sneaker, leaving some areas unpainted.

2 To make the second colour add more paint to the mixture to produce a beige. Repeat step 1 (above) with the second colour, filling in some of the unpainted areas on each sneaker.

3 Make a third colour by adding more red and brown paint to the mixture. Repeat step 1 again to fill in the remaining unpainted areas. Do not worry if the vertical stripes overlap the first two colours — this will add to the overall finished effect.

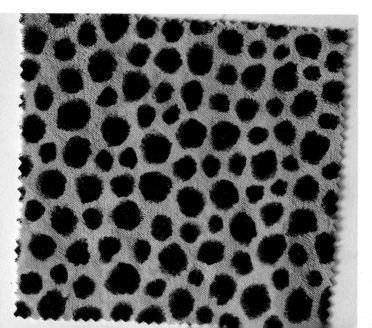

4 Leave background colour to dry. Then, using black fabric paint or a fabric pen, add the markings by painting irregular spots all over the surface.

5 When the paint is thoroughly dry, wipe off any excess paint that has run on to the rubber of the sneaker sole using a clean cloth dipped in water. If there are any remaining dark blotches, paint over them with white paint.

Stencilling on fabric

*Stencilling on fabric has become an exciting
technique that is within the reach of everyone. You do not have to
be an expert to transform a room by stencilling curtains
and cushions to match walls and furniture, or to produce colourful
and co-ordinated clothes and fashion accessories.*

*▽ Stencilling lets you transfer your own ideas to
fabric: here it adds fruit to the work of the loom.*

Materials and equipment

You will need special brushes and paints for fabric stencilling, but the expense is worthwhile, especially if you intend to do a lot of this sort of work, because both paints and brushes last a long time.

Paints

In order to stencil on fabric successfully, the paint you use must be thick enough not to run or to be absorbed by the material. There are special, permanent, fabric paints available from art supply shops and these come in a wide range of colours and a choice of finishes — opaque, transparent or pearlized. Some stencil paints are multi-purpose and can be used on fabrics as well as hard surfaces, so check the manufacturer's instructions.

Certain fabric dyes come with a special thickener which can be mixed with the colours, giving them a paint-like consistency, making them suitable for stencilling. Again, check the instructions to make sure they are what you want.

Remember that some brands of fabric paint require heat fixing with a domestic iron.

Ordinary cans of spray paint can also be used on fabric. These are washable, but because they stiffen the fabric they are only suitable for certain soft furnishings, such as drapes, blinds and curtains. They are not good for clothes.

Fabric paints, fabric dyes and stencil paints are all available from art and craft shops.

Brushes

You will need a special stencil brush, as used for stencilling on walls, with the bristles cut squarely to create a firm, flat end for applying the paint. Ideally, use a separate brush for each colour. When not in use, store the brushes with an elastic band around the bristles to help keep their shape.

Diffusers

For a fine, smooth finish, you can apply stencilled colour with a diffuser. This is a simple device that enables you, literally, to blow the paint on to the fabric, so spreading the tiny droplets to create an even, precise area of flat colour. The diffuser is made up of two tubular sections: one end of the diffuser is placed in the paint container while you blow into the other end, thus creating a vacuum. The paint is forced out through a small nozzle at the joint of the two sections. Diffusers are available from art and graphic supply shops. When using a diffuser, fabric paints must be diluted with an equal quantity of water to prevent clogging.

An alternative diffuser is a good-quality plant mister. Provided the paint is the correct consistency, and you do a few practice pieces, this cheaper and more readily available alternative may be the best one. You will need a separate plant mister for each colour.

The consistency of the paint should be thinner when using a diffuser than with a stenciling brush. It is best to build up the colour in thin layers to avoid soaking the fabric with paint.

Sponges

Paint can also be applied to the fabric with either a synthetic or natural sponge. Cut the sponge into small pieces, using a different piece for each colour. By using a sponge you will create a more subtle, textured finish than with a brush or diffuser.

Fabrics

Natural fibres, such as cotton, linen, calico and silk, are ideal for stencilling, but you can also stencil on washable synthetics. Flimsy materials, such as organdy and chiffon, must be stretched taut and taped down before being stencilled. Water-repellent and oily fibres are difficult, and should be avoided, as should heavily textured and woolly materials. All fabrics should be well washed, to remove any dressing, and then ironed.

When stencilling two-sided items such as cushion covers and T-shirts, place a piece of board or plastic between the layers of fabric to prevent paint seeping through.

Stencils

Any good-quality stencil can be used on fabrics. For coarser materials it is best to choose a fairly simple design, as the lines and details of a complicated pattern will be lost when they are broken up by the weave of the fabric.

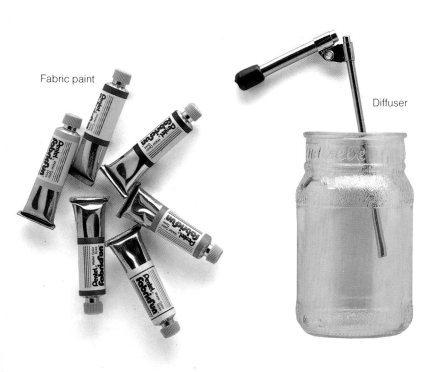

Fabric paint

Diffuser

Plant mister

Applying the colour

1 Wash the fabric to remove any dressing and dirt. Iron to remove creases. Stretch the fabric, or the part of the fabric to be stencilled, over a padded table or board and stick in place with masking tape. Place the stencil in position, holding it in place with tape if necessary.

2 Stipple the colour working from the edges inwards. If using a brush, hold this upright and apply colour in a circular motion. Moisten the bristles first by dragging them across a damp cloth. It is important not to wet the brush too much as this will over-dilute the colours and cause them to run into the fabric. Dip the tips of the bristles only into the paint, and remove any excess by wiping the bristles across a dry cloth or towel.

3 If using a sponge, this should be barely damp. Be careful not to overload the sponge with paint as this will cause a build up of paint on the fabric.

4 If using a diffuser, direct the nozzle end toward the fabric, and blow through the mouthpiece. It is best to practise on a piece of spare material first, just to get the technique right. The layer of paint will be fine but let it dry before applying another to deepen the colour.

5 Whichever method you use to apply the paint, allow the first colour to dry completely before applying a second and subsequent colours. When you have applied the final colour and the paint is dry, remove the stencil and fix the colours with a hot iron if necessary (see manufacturer's instructions).

TIP   COLOUR SHADING

The absorbency of fabric makes it difficult to get a shaded effect simply by applying the paint more thickly to the shadow area.

To shade your stencilled design, apply the first colour as flatly and opaquely as possible and allow this to dry.

For the shading, choose a darker colour or a darker tone of the same colour and, holding the stencil in the same position, stipple around the edge of the shape. Gradually lighten the pressure on the brush, blending the shading colour into the under colour.

Corner stencil motif

Stencilled borders can be effective on curtains, cushion covers, table cloths, napkins, bedspreads and other soft furnishings. On items such as these, the corners are particularly important because they are often conspicuous. For this pretty border, follow the instructions for stencilling on fabric and use the corner motif shown here.

You will need
◇ Table cloth, napkins or other fabric item
◇ Fabric paints
◇ Stencil pattern
◇ Card or acetate stencil material
◇ Pencil, tracing paper and craft knife
◇ Brush, diffuser or sponge
◇ Tape

Corner motif

There are several ways of coping with a stencilled corner, depening on the type of border you are using. Mitring is suitable for many border designs. However, it is often neater and more effective to use a separate corner motif. The motif should normally be fairly compact and should be based on a circle or an equal-sided figure, such as a square or octagon.

The corner motif shown here is a perfect solution. Trace the corner motif and cut out the stencil. When stencilling around corners, mark out the position of the border first. Position and stencil the corner motifs, ensuring they are equally spaced. Then stencil the border itself. This can either be chosen to match the corner motif, or it can be an unrelated shape.

Stencilled floor mat

*Individual, attractive and practical, a
stencilled canvas mat makes a wonderful alternative to a carpet
or rug for a kitchen, bathroom or hallway. Not only
will it add comfort and beauty, it will also exclude draughts and
provide a smooth, easy-to-clean surface.*

A properly primed, stencilled and varnished floor mat stands up to everyday wear and tear extremely well, even on stairs. It is quite a time-consuming project but is fun to do and is a very cost-effective way of covering a floor.

Materials and equipment

Frame To achieve a professional finish the canvas should be stretched over a wooden frame be-fore it is primed and painted. The frame makes the canvas easier to work on and enables the mat to be stowed away while the paint dries.

Canvas Artists' supply shops sell a good selection of canvas. Buy a closely woven canvas the size you want the floor mat to be, plus at least 6in (15cm) extra all round for attaching it to the frame and, later, for trimming and finishing.

Primer, made from white glue and acrylic paint, protects the canvas and provides a smooth and supple surface for stencilling. White glue is available from most artists' suppliers and some hardware stores or builders' merchants.

Varnish Four thin coats of varnish should be enough. If the varnish mixture is too thick, or too many layers are added, the colours will darken, as even 'clear' varnishes have a rather yellowish cast.

Making a stencilled mat

The key to making a successful stencilled mat is to prepare the canvas properly by stretching it on a frame and priming it well. Before starting to paint, practise stencilling your chosen design on a piece of paper. And finally, the decorated canvas must be varnished.

Preparing the stencil

Use a shop-bought stencil or design your own stencil pattern, cutting it out of acetate. The design could be a simple motif or a more complicated repeat pattern. Stripes and checked patterns are easy to achieve using masking tape.

Making a frame

Make the frame by gluing and nailing the battens together. Reinforce each corner with a right-angled metal bracket to ensure that the frame is firm.

Preparing the canvas

1 If necessary, trim the canvas. Stretch it over the frame and secure it tightly using either tacks or a staple gun.

2 Mix 3½pts (2l) latex paint with 18fl oz (500ml) white glue. Using large brush, paint on three coats of primer, allowing paint to dry between each coat. After the third coat has dried, sand the surface to ensure that it is smooth.

3 Apply two more coats of primer, sanding lightly between each layer. Then paint the underside of the canvas with a couple of coats of primer. Leave the canvas to dry thoroughly.

Stencilling

Mix approximately 2tbsp of artists' acrylic paint on a saucer. If necessary, mix two colours together to achieve a different colour. With very little paint on the stencil brush, test the colour by dabbing the brush on a piece of paper. Once you are satisfied with the effect, begin to stencil the canvas. If using more than one colour, wait until the first colour has dried before applying the next.

Finishing touches

1 Thin the first two coats of varnish with mineral spirits – mix three parts varnish to one part mineral spirits. For subsequent coats mix four parts varnish to one part mineral spirits.

2 Quickly and sparingly paint on the varnish using a large paint brush. Leave to dry for at least 6-8 hours between each coat. Protect the underside of the floor mat with a couple of coats of varnish. The more coats applied, the tougher the surface.

3 Once the varnish is dry, remove the canvas from the frame. Trim the edges of the canvas, leaving a 2in (5cm) allowance all round. Snip the corners neatly so that they will mitre together, then fold edges to underside of that.

4 Stick the edges down using white glue (choose one that remains flexible when dry and will not stain the canvas).

TIP   BASE COLOUR

For a coloured background, tint the primer with acrylic paint between steps 2 and 3 of preparing the canvas. Two coats of paint will produce a light background; for a darker tint use three coats of paint. Lightly sand the canvas between each coat.

Geometric mat

This eye-catching geometric pattern is reminiscent of decorative tiles. The completed size of the mat is $36\frac{3}{4}$ x 26in (93 x 66cm). If you wish to make a larger or smaller mat, adjust the design accordingly.

You will need

◇ Four $1\frac{1}{2}$in (38mm) square wooden battens, two 34in (86cm) long, two 45in (114cm) long
◇ 2in (5cm) nails
◇ Wood glue
◇ Four small right-angled metal brackets for corners of frame
◇ Screws
◇ Firmly woven canvas at least 49 x 38in (124.5 x 96.5cm)
◇ Tacks or a staple gun
◇ Emulsion latex
◇ White glue
◇ Large household paint brush and stencil brushes
◇ Medium grade sandpaper
◇ Masking tape
◇ Acetate
◇ Pencil and a ruler
◇ Utility knife or sharp craft knife
◇ Acrylic paints in green and red
◇ Polyurethane varnish

Method

1 Make the frame and stretch and prime canvas as described on previous page.

2 On separate sheets of acetate trace the border stencil twice. Using a sharp craft knife, cut away sections to be green on first tracing. On second tracing, cut away sections to be red. Repeat for the corner stencil.

3 Using a triangle, draw a rectangle 21 x $10\frac{3}{8}$in (53 x 26cm) on paper. Cut out rectangle to use as template. Centre template on canvas and, with a ruler and pencil, lightly but accurately mark a rectangle of same size – this is the guide for green stencil.

4 Position the green stencil so that the arrow marked 'start' lines up with one outer corner of the pencil rectangle. The top cut edge of the stencil must lie completely flush with the pencil line. Using the green acrylic paint, stencil the first motif as given. Allow to dry thoroughly.

5 Move the stencil along so that the side butts up to the adjoining motif and the top edge is again flush with the pencil line. Stencil and allow to dry. Repeat twice to complete one side.

6 Repeat steps 3 and 4 for remaining three sides, stencilling two motifs only at the narrow ends. Position the green corner section in each corner and stencil. Allow the green paint to dry.

7 Using green motifs as guide to positioning, stencil red sections with red paint. Allow to dry.

8 Mask off the outer sections of green stencil and stencil three green motifs in the centre of mat.

9 Use masking tape to mark red borders. Position tape to just cover edge of green border. For centre border, position strip of tape 1in (2.5cm) from green edge. Then mask 2in (5cm) out from outer green edge. Stencil borders in red. When paint has dried, remove tape and complete the mat as shown.

STENCIL TEMPLATES

Start

Border stencil ▶

◀ Corner stencil

Painting sheer fabric

*Paint semi-transparent fabric with bright and
colourful designs to produce a subtle, yet elegant effect, which
is further enhanced when light is allowed to filter
through the fabric. This is an excellent way of transforming
plain fabrics into unique designer textiles.*

Sheer and semi-sheer fabrics, painted with striking, vibrantly coloured designs, can be successfully used to make home furnishings, such as curtains or wall hangings, or items of clothing, like elegant blouses. Curtains made from painted sheer fabrics look particularly good as they allow the light from outside to shine through the fabric, revealing areas of opaque colour alongside more translucent colour.

Choosing fabrics

Different types, weights and weaves of fabric can greatly affect the colour intensity of the fabric paint. Always experiment with test pieces of spare fabric before tackling the main project. This will enable you to check the finished paint effect and make any necessary adjustments to the consistency of the paint before you start. Allow the paint to dry before judging the colour.

△ *These sheer and semi-transparent painted fabrics give an idea of the shimmering effects you can achieve.*

Although silk is a wonderful fabric to work with — producing lovely, shimmering paint effects — it can be rather expensive to use for large items. Therefore, in this chapter we concentrate on working with less expensive sheer fabrics made from cotton and polyester.

Natural fabrics, such as cotton, are definitely the most suitable to use as they absorb paints and dyes extremely well, producing bright, vivid colours. However, successful results can also be achieved with man-made fabrics, such as polyester; although the fabric does not absorb the paint as well as natural fabrics, it is much easier to achieve an even finish and the colours blend very well.

Here we have used three fabrics: cotton organdie, cotton voile and sheer polyester.

Organdie is a fairly crisp, semi-transparent cotton fabric.

Cotton voile is a soft, plain-weave, semi-transparent fabric. It hangs well and can be used to great effect for draping at windows.

Sheer polyester is virtually transparent and takes the paint well, giving soft and subtle, muted colours. The advantage of using polyester is that it is much cheaper than natural fabrics.

Painting sheer fabric

The brilliant colours and strong geometric design of the motif used to decorate this sheer fabric are made all the more effective when emphasized with a gutta outline. The gutta separates the motif areas of opaque colour from the wash of diluted paint used to colour the background area. For further information on using clear and coloured gutta, see pages 115-118, 127-128 and 133-134.

▷ *Coloured gutta has been used to outline this motif. Trace the design on to a sheet of paper to use as a template.*

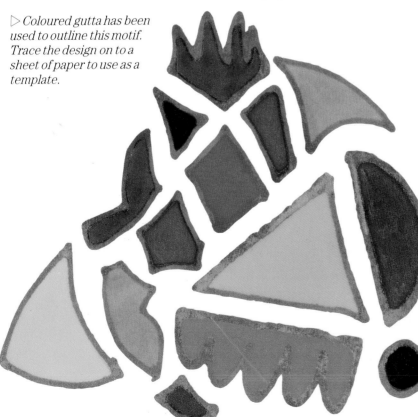

You will need

◇ Sheer or semi-sheer cotton voile, organdie or polyester
◇ Wooden frame and silk pins
◇ Paper
◇ Felt tip pen or pencil
◇ Fabric paints: we used lemon yellow, golden yellow, pink, Orient red, carmine red, French blue, brilliant green, orange, black and turquoise.
◇ Gutta and applicator bottle (for thicker design lines use a small, fine paint brush)
◇ Small paint brushes to apply motif colours
◇ Two 1in (2.5cm) wide soft paint brushes, to apply the background colours and to blend the colours
◇ Diffuser or plant spray

Method

1 Wash the fabric to remove any manufacturer's finishes. Leave to dry; then iron it. Stretch the fabric over the wooden frame and secure in place with silk pins.

2 Using a felt tip pen or pencil, trace the motif on to a piece of paper which can be used beneath the fabric as a template from which to trace the design outline.

3 Draw the motif design on to the fabric using gutta, taking care not to allow the fabric to touch the paper as staining could occur. Repeat over the entire area. Allow the gutta to dry thoroughly.

4 Using a small paint brush, fill in the motif with your chosen fabric paint colours, making sure you have enough of each colour to complete all the motifs. Allow each colour to dry before applying the next. To achieve the effects in our samples do not dilute the colours. When finished, allow to dry.

5 Mix up the colour, or colours, for the background wash by mixing one part paint to one part water for each colour used, ensuring that you mix enough to cover the whole area. Two colours will give a more varied look.

6 Using a diffuser or plant mister, spray a light mist of clean water over the entire surface of the fabric. (It is essential to keep the fabric damp when applying the background colours, to achieve an even finish — especially when using cotton fabrics, which absorb paint well. Dampen the fabric again if it dries out.)

7 Using a large soft brush and, working as quickly as you can, cover as much of the background as possible, swapping colours if using several. Then, with a small paint brush, carefully but still quickly, paint around the tricky areas of designs. Blend in the colours and even out any patchy areas using a large, soft brush and clean water. Leave to dry, there is no need to remove it from the frame.

8 Remove the fabric from the frame and fix the paint, following the manufacturer's instructions. Wash the fabric in warm soapy water to remove the gutta. Leave to dry thoroughly.

TIP ◆	COLOURED GUTTA

As a variation of this design use a coloured gutta. As the sample (shown left) reveals, it can alter the overall look quite significantly.

Painting on silk basics

*Painting on silk enables you to achieve
beautiful, translucent effects simply and quickly. Even if you
are not a skilled artist, you can create exquisite
cushions and wall hangings to adorn your home, or scarves and
clothes to wear for special occasions.*

△ *Geometric designs are painted on to lengths of silk which are sewn to make cushion covers or simply tied over cushion pads to enliven the room with splashes of colour.*

The simple methods for painting on silk allow you to copy favourite patterns or make 'free' designs by painting on waves or stripes of colour and allowing it to blend at the edges. As silk takes colour so well, vibrant effects can be created easily. There are two techniques for painting on silk and each gives a different effect to the finished product.

Gutta or 'block' method

Defined shapes are created by outlining every colour area with a blocking solution to stop colours running into each other. It is normally used in a transparent form but is also available in colours.

Watercolour method

Paint applied directly to silk always runs so that different colour areas merge into one another. This method gives the effect of a watercolour painting. You can add textures to enhance your design simply by using alcohol, salt and sugar.

Materials and equipment

Everything you need for painting on silk is available from craft shops. And silk can be bought from most department stores or fabric shops.

Silk

Silk comes in a variety of textures and thicknesses. Avoid coarse or patterned weaves unless you want a textured effect. Choose white silk as paint colours are affected by the colour of the fabric background. All types of silk must be washed before painting to remove the dressing applied by the manufacturers.

△ *Outlining your design with gutta allows you to create defined colour areas.*

△ *Use the watercolour method to create colour areas that merge into one another.*

Pongee, sometimes sold as Jap silk or Habutai, is an even-weave silk that is cheaper than other types. Its smooth surface makes it ideal for all silk painting techniques.

Crêpe de chine and satin are soft with delicate textures. Like pongee, they are suitable for all silk painting techniques, although slightly more difficult to handle.

Paints

Silk paints are either water or alcohol based. Both come in thin liquid form but the two types differ in the way they are fixed and it is therefore essential not to mix the two. To be certain of a uniform result, use the same brand of paint, gutta and fixing agent when working on the same design.

Silk paints come in a wide range of colours but you need only a few to start with. You can mix colours or create a pastel version of each colour by diluting it with water or a lightening agent, depending on the brand of paint you are using.

Brushes

You will need a selection of brushes, including a fine brush for narrow lines and a broad brush for filling in large areas. Silk painting brushes, available in craft shops, have specially bound bristles which enable them to hold a lot of colour at one time. However, artist's brushes are also suitable if you choose a soft, natural bristle such as sable or squirrel.

Frame

A frame for stretching the silk is essential. Either buy a ready-made frame from a craft shop or make your own with four pieces of planed wood. Alternatively, you can improvize by using an old picture frame, provided it is sturdy.

Pins for stretching the silk must be fine or they will tear the fabric. Three-pronged craft pins are ideal, otherwise use push-pins or long-pointed thumbtacks.

Gutta

If you want to create an image with clear outlines on silk then you must use gutta which is a blocking agent. This prevents different paint colours running into each other. You can also use gutta to block out whole areas: the parts coated with gutta repel any colour painted over them so that they retain the colour of the fabric.

There are several types of gutta,

TIP GUTTA APPLICATOR

Gutta can be applied with a cone made from tracing paper or greaseproof paper.

1 Cut a rectangle measuring 23 x 18cm (9 x 7in), roll into a cone and secure with sticky tape.

2 Fill the cone with gutta, roll up the end and fix with a paper clip.

Gutta method

1 Tape the silk on to a flat surface and sketch the design with a pencil or a special fabric marker that washes out. To trace a design, put the original under the silk and trace the outline.

2 Stretch the silk across the frame and pin it in position. Fit the gutta bottle with a nozzle or prepare an alternative applicator. Apply the gutta along the drawn outline. There should be no breaks in the gutta line otherwise the paint will seep through. Allow the gutta to dry.

3 Apply the paint to the silk with a watercolour brush, beginning in the middle of each colour area. Because the paint spreads there is no need to risk taking it right up to the edge of the shape, so stop just short of the gutta outline. Work quickly to get a smooth finish and never go back and paint over a dry area as this will create a tidemark. Allow the paint to dry and then fix it by following the manufacturer's instructions for the fixing agent you are using.

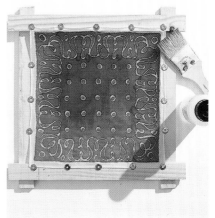

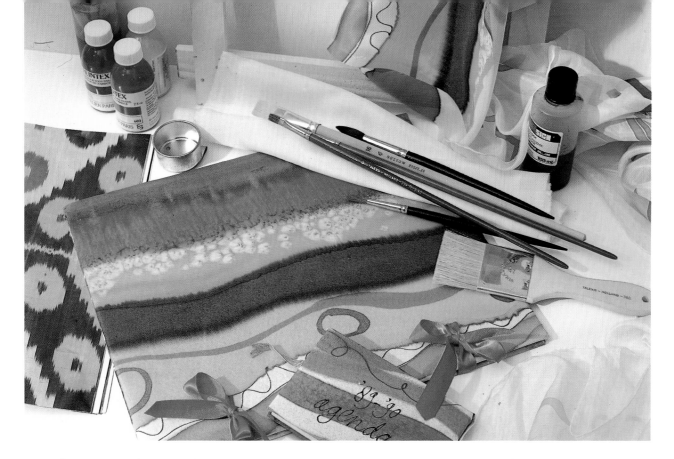

so make sure you buy one that is compatible with your paints. Ask a supplier if you are not sure. You may also need a thinner to dilute the gutta as it tends to thicken. Again, ask your supplier for the correct type to go with your paints.

Some brands of gutta come in plastic bottles with nozzles that can be pierced to form applicators. Others come in bottles to which nozzles of different sizes can be fitted according to the line thickness desired. Another option is to use a plastic pipette.

△ All you need is white silk, paints, brushes, gutta and a frame and you are ready to start painting on silk. Once you have mastered the techniques you will be able to make a variety of colourful designs. Try using experimental patterns to cover folders and books.

Watercolour method

Stretch and pin the silk on to the frame ensuring that the fabric is taut but not overstretched. When painting on to the silk, bear in mind that the colour spreads — paint stripes and shapes smaller than you want them. For flowing, runny designs brush the silk with thinner or water (depending on the manufacturer's instructions for the brand of paint you are using) before starting to paint.

Creating textures

Many images are enhanced if they are given a subtle texture. And it is simple to add interest to your finished piece using ordinary household substances.

Using salt and sugar

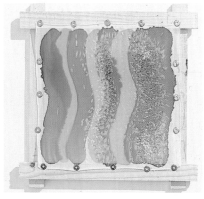

To create a granular or mottled texture, sprinkle salt or sugar on to the wet paint and wait until it is dry before removing the grains with a dry brush. Rock salt is used here to create a coarse texture; table salt and sugar give a subtler, stippled effect.

Using alcohol

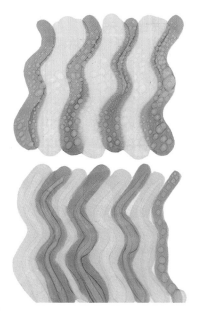

Marbled and mottled textures can be created with alcohol. Use a cotton swab, to dab on denatured alcohol, or surgical spirit to areas of dry colour where you want to lighten the colour. After the textured areas are dry, you can add further colour on top of them.

DESIGN LIBRARY

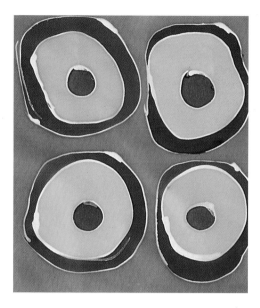

◁ *Wavy lines of gutta are drawn on to the silk and followed by stripes of bold colour.*

▷ *Try drawing circles freehand on to the silk with gutta and filling in with vibrant colours.*

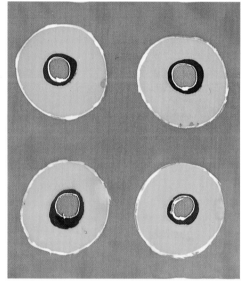

◁ *Simple yellow circles with a turquoise centre have an Aztec look.*

▷ *Freehand zigzag lines are filled in with colour, with one zigzag left startling white.*

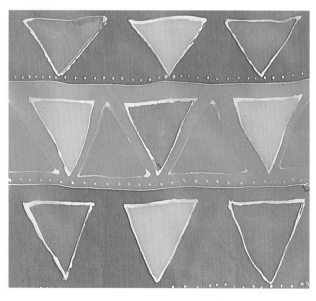

△ *A harmonious colour scheme of turquoise blue, jade, citrus green and yellow is the ideal complement for this geometric design.*

△ *A patchwork of contrasting colours looks cheerful. Applying the gutta in simple flowing lines enhances the effect of the motif.*

Mixing colours

*Beautiful colours and stunning designs
are not just for the experts. By following a few simple rules
and understanding a little about the principles of
making and matching colours, you can mix your own dyes to
paint these lovely silk scarves.*

Although most silk dyes come in a wide range of colours, it is handy to know how to mix your own colours. Having this skill not only puts a limitless range of colours at your fingertips, it means real savings. By investing in just the few key colours it is possible to mix any colour in the spectrum. These skills can be applied to any form of painting, from mixing household paints for your walls to dyeing or painting your shoes a new colour !

Basic colour theory also helps to explain how colours work together and this is a very useful design tool. By understanding colours and their relationship with one another it is possible to create more effective colour schemes. This skill can be applied to more that just painting. It will help when it comes to choosing colours for an embroidery, planning a colour scheme for a room or picking the colours for a silk scarf, as on these pages.

▽ *These beautiful, painted silk scarves show how colours can be successfully mixed and used.*

Introducing colours

Without light there would be no colour, as colour is formed by light waves reflecting off objects. Pass pure white light, such as sunlight, through a prism and you will see the entire spectrum of colours — the colours of a rainbow. Every surface absorbs light and reflects back only part of the spectrum. So a blue object is one that reflects back only blue light and absorbs all the other colours of light.

All colours can be mixed from three basic colours, called primaries. The colours that are mixed from primaries are called secondary colours. When secondary colours are mixed with primaries they form tertiary colours. These colours, and all the other hues of the spectrum, are called pure colours because they do not contain any white or black.

Primary colours

Yellow, blue and a pink-red (magenta) are the true primary colours, so-called because they cannot be mixed from any other colours. In theory, you can create any other colour from the three primaries; but this can be time-consuming. In practice, it is quicker and easier to start off with a few more manufactured colours.

Harmony

A harmonious colour scheme is one in which the colours work well together, and in which no single colour dominates or clashes with the others. The simplest way to create harmony in a colour scheme is to select colours which lie next to each other on the colour wheel; green, blue and turquoise, for example, work well together. For a warmer harmonious colour scheme choose reds, yellows and oranges.

Contrasting colours

The colours that lie opposite each other on the basic colour wheel are known as complementary colours, namely: orange and blue; green and red; yellow and violet. Each pair offer the strongest contrast between colours because each one contains no trace of its complement.

For the silk painter this piece of theory is also extremely useful. Complementary or contrasting colour schemes are much more exciting than harmonious ones, and they can be used to great effect in textile designs. But make sure the

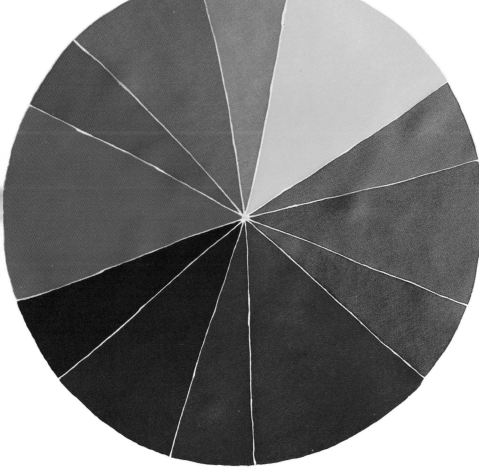

The colour wheel

The colours of the spectrum, from yellow through to blue, can form a complete circle, with each colour progressing to the next. This circle is known as a colour wheel. A basic colour wheel shows the primary and secondary colours. Each secondary colour is sandwiched between the two primaries it is mixed from.

A colour wheel is the best way of illustrating the way colours relate to each other. The position of colours

△ *This colour wheel helps show the relationship between the primary, secondary and tertiary colours.*

on the wheel will show whether they blend harmoniously together (as with colours that are close together), or contrast (which happens with colours that are opposite each other on the wheel). It is important to understand the role of harmonious and contrasting colours.

Secondary colours

The secondary colours are those mixed from the three primaries: mix yellow and magenta together to produce orange; mix yellow and blue together to make green; and violet is produced by mixing magenta with blue. The primary and secondary colours make up the main colours of the spectrum.

Tertiary colours

A tertiary colour is one mixed from a primary and a secondary colour. The tertiary colours are orange-yellow, orange-red, violet-red, violet-blue, green-blue and green-yellow.

colours are used in workable proportions. If used in identical amounts, the colours will 'fight' with each other. It is much more pleasing to use one as an accent colour for the other; for example, a green-based design with a splash of red or vivid pink. Used in this way, contrasting colours can create a vibrant, eye-catching colour scheme.

Clashing colours

The colour wheel not only shows how to choose harmonious colours; it can also be used to create more interesting colour schemes. Our eye expects to see colours in the logical progression of the colour wheel; for example, red to be darker than orange. When this natural order is reversed, such as pink put with orange, we react with a jolt as it is not what we expect to see. This is why some colours appear to clash.

Another form of contrasting or clashing colours is created by reversing the expected tones of complementary colours. For instance, we expect purple to be darker than yellow. When this is reversed and a pale mauve is put with yellow it looks discordant. Pale blue with orange, or pink with green, also create the same uncomfortable feeling. Discordant colours, when used in the correct proportions, form another useful design tool.

Cool and warm colours

All colours have a 'temperature' which affects how we react to them. Some colours can make us feel hot, while others cause us to shiver. These reactions are caused largely by association; thus the warm colours are red, orange and yellow, because they remind us of heat and sun. Blue, green and violet are cool, because we associate them with water and shade.

Warm colours are generally more dominant in a design, and seem to jump out from the rest. Cooler col-

ours tend to merge and recede. For instance, if you paint a red square next to a green one, the red one always looks as if it is more prominent than the green one.

There is no reason why warm and cool colours can't be used together, but it is important to get a balance between the two. Never let the stronger colours overpower the others. Alternatively, you might prefer to restrict your design to one colour temperature, using all cool colours or all warm colours.

Tones

For each colour there is a tonal equivalent, somewhere on the scale between very light grey and very dark grey. To decide the tone of a colour, try to imagine how it would look in a black and white photograph. The closer it is to white, the

lighter the grey, or tone. Therefore, any pale colours, such as lemon or lilac, and tonally light; and deep reds and blues are tonally dark. An effective design must include a good balance of tones to create depth and interest.

Tints and shades

All of the colours on the colour wheel can be made darker or lighter by adding black or white. A pale version of a colour, when white is added to lighten it, is known as a tint. A deep version of a colour, when black is added to it, is referred to as a shade. Hence, 'light' red, or pink, is a tint, and 'dark' red is a shade.

With silk dyes, a shade is created by mixing a little black with a colour. But, for a tint, you need to add a little water or proprietary dilutent to lighten the colour.

Neutrals

Elegant neutral colours are always popular, either on their own or to set off a splash of a brighter colour. The neutrals, which include grey, beiges and some browns, can all be mixed from the primary and the secondary colours.

Grey is the most popular neutral colour, and there are various ways of mixing this, the most usual being a combination of black and white.

With dyes, however, there is no white. Therefore, grey is produced by diluting black, either with water or with a proprietary thinner, depending on the brand. The more you dilute the black, the paler the grey you will be left with.

There are, however, several other ways of mixing grey with different combinations of almost all colours. The greys shown here are all mixed from the primary colours, and you can see how each grey is slightly biased towards a primary: in this way you can produce a yellowy-grey by mixing slightly more yellow with the blue and red; or a reddish-grey by adding slightly more red, and so on. Some of the most beautiful and subtle silk paintings have been produced using different greys, with no other colours.

Starter kit

The secondary colours we get from mixing two true primaries are not the only versions of violet, green and orange. If you mix a different red with a different blue, the resulting violet will not be the same as the violet on the colour wheel.

When investing in a basic range of dyes or paints, a good choice is: warm red and magenta; deep blue, like indigo, and the true blue; lemon yellow and gold yellow. By starting with these colours it is possible to mix a wide range of secondary and tertiary colours.

TIP   MIXING COLOURS

Follow this tip for mixing secondary colours successfully:
Gold yellow mixed with warm red to make orange.
Lemon yellow mixed with true blue to produce a strong green.
Magenta mixed with deep blue to make purple.

Planning colours

By mixing your own dyes it is possible to
paint a customized scarf that will co-ordinate with
any item in your wardrobe. Try to colour match
an existing printed garment, or develop an exciting new
colour scheme using the ideas shown here.

Silk painting is a very pleasurable hobby — even more so when you gain the confidence to mix your own dyes and create your own colour schemes. Working with colour, once a few basic principles are understood, is very rewarding.

Colour, and people's response to it, is a very personal thing — we all know what colours we do and don't

like. However, in general, our response to colour is guided by association. Consequently the reds, oranges and yellows are perceived as warm colours — because they remind us of the sun and fire; blues and greens are cool like the sea, while neutrals offer a restful mood.

Before you start to plan your colour scheme decide on the mood

△ *These cool harmonious colours of blue, violet, pink and purple work particularly well on a dark green background because it provides a different tone to the floral motifs.*

you want to create; should it be cool harmonious and soothing — or are bold, vibrant, clashing colours more to taste? Some colour schemes are easier to create than others. Neutral, harmonious and tonal schemes rarely present problems, so it may be best to start designing with one of these. Clashing and contrasting colour schemes are harder to design effectively, but they are exciting and challenging.

Whichever scheme and mood you choose it is important to remember these factors.

Importance of tone

An effective design will include a wide range of tones. This is easy to develop if working in one colour, but harder if a number of colours are used. Refer to the tonal chart in the previous section as a guideline and try to include colours that have both dark, light and medium tones in your design.

▽ *Here oranges, reds and yellows have been combined with a deep beige to create an example of a warm, harmonious scheme.*

Importance of balance

The balance of the colours in the pattern is crucial — especially when working with contrasting and clashing schemes. As a rule some colours should dominate, while others are used in much smaller proportions. The position of the colours should also be balanced across the design.

Planning

It is very difficult to imagine what colours will look like together, so experiment first. Keep mixing the colours and painting them on a scrap of paper until you are content with the way they work. Then keep 'colouring in' a small copy of your design until you are pleased with the placement of the colours. Only then paint your scarf.

△ *Unexpected colours often make the most effective colour themes. Here the reds, browns and deep clarets are harmonious, while the deep green leaves form an interesting, reduced contrast to the claret stems. The vibrant green is discordant to the darker reds.*

Painting a scarf

Each of the scarves shown on these pages is the same design — just painted in different colour schemes. Study the way these colours work to help you plan your own colour scheme. The finished scarf is 26in (66cm) square.

You will need

◇ 1yd (90cm) silk
◇ A silk painting frame
◇ Clear gutta
◇ A selection of brushes
◇ Silk paints in the following colours for mixing: red, magenta, deep gold yellow, lemon yellow, mid blue, deep blue and black
◇ Old jars for mixing the colours
◇ Old spoon or stick for stirring the colours
◇ Scraps of silk to practise with
◇ Fixing agent to set dyes (see dye manufacturer's instructions)
◇ Paper, pencil and ruler

Preparing to paint

Enlarge the graph to the correct size and prepare the screen. See page 116.

Before you start

Mix up your colours and plan the placement of the colours as described on the previous page.

▽ *The basis of this design is warm, harmonious colours but it has been given extra punch by the addition of touches of blue — the complementary to orange. Deep grey gives the design a greater tonal range, adding extra interest.*

Painting the scarf

The scarf has been painted using the gutta method (see pages 116-118).

Cool harmonious colours

By restricting your choice to the colours on the 'cool' side of the wheel, such as blue, green and violet, you can automatically create a sense of harmony in a design. Avoid any colours which may be verging on the warm side; some blues or violets can contain quite a large proportion of a warm colour, such as pinky mauves or lemon greens. Cool colours help to evoke a feeling of tranquillity and calm.

Warm harmonious colours

The warm colours, red, orange and yellow, enhance each other and work well together. Too many warm colours can be overpowering so try toning the more primary colours down with warm autumnal colours like mustard and ochre.

Contrasting colours

The contrasting or complementary colours — violet and yellow, orange and blue, or red and green — provide a useful basis for many designs. Use all three of these combinations or, alternatively, limit your design to a single pair.

Remember you are not restricted to using unmixed colours. For instance, a design based on orange and green could contain many different coloured greens and oranges, as well as neutral colours obtained by mixing the two together.

Whether you are using a limited range or a wide selection of colours, remember that the most successful colour combinations are created using different shades and tints. It is also important that one of the colours dominates. Use, for instance, a predominantly green scheme, with splashes of orange.

Clashing colours

These colour schemes should be handled with great care, and the same rule applies here as for contrasts — if the colours are used in equal proportions they may end up looking sickly and disturbing. But if one dominates, relieved by a touch of a clashing or discordant colour, then the effect can be very stunning indeed.

Tones

It is important to be aware of the tonal value of the colours you use and of how these are arranged in the design. If you are using both light and dark colours, try and arrange these so that the tones fall in an interesting way.

Again, try to imagine the design photographed in black and white. This will help you to compare the

△ *Tones of greens through to a pale greeny beige, set against an inky green/grey background, create a pleasing scheme. The subtleness of the colours lend the scarf sophistication.*

depths of each different colour in association with the others being used in the design.

◁ *This chart only shows the actual design area of the scarf. In order to mount the silk on a frame, it is necessary to add at least 6in (15cm) extra to the outer edge of the scarf. To enlarge the graph, transfer the grid on to a piece of paper. Take care to mark the centres on the grid as this will make it easier to map out the design lines. Alternatively, enlarge the design on a photocopier. When the paper pattern is ready, position it under the silk, and use a sharp pencil to lightly trace the design on to the silk.*

1 square = ³/₈in (1cm)

Painting on silk

*This exotic, tropical bird pattern is ideal for a
scarf, cushion or wall hanging. Choose brilliant colours to
match the subject or be adventurous and mix your own
from a small selection of paints, picking a colour scheme to
enhance an outfit or to complement a room.*

The gutta technique described in the previous section is used to create this decorative silk square. Although the design looks complicated, it is made up of areas of flat colour and so is actually quite simple to paint even if you are not a skilled artist.

Preparing the pattern

On a 36in (90cm) square of paper, enlarge the diagram to the correct size as shown by the key. The enlarged pattern measures 35¼in (88cm) square. Once the grid is drawn, the design is easy to copy.

Painting the design
You will need

◇ White silk square 36in (90cm)
◇ Gutta
◇ Fixer
◇ Frame, pins
◇ Pencil
◇ Paints
◇ Gutta applicator
◇ Paintbrushes
◇ Tape

1 Hand wash the silk in warm water mixed with mild detergent to remove the dressing applied by the manufacturers. Allow the silk to dry naturally and then press it with an iron.

2 Place the paper pattern on a flat surface and tape the silk in position over it. The fabric is slightly larger than the pattern to allow a ½in (1cm) hem all round. Using a sharp pencil, lightly trace the design on to the silk.

3 Stretch and pin the silk on to the frame. Apply the gutta, following the outline of the drawn design with the gutta nozzle. It is best to start at the top of the design and work downwards so as not to smudge the wet gutta. Check the gutta outline carefully as it is important to fill in any gaps to prevent the paint bleeding.

4 As all brands of silk paint come in many colours you should be able to find the right shades to match an outfit or the decor of a room. An economical option is to mix your own colours. With a little practice, you will be able to create any colour you

want so, instead of buying a whole range of paints, try starting with a few basic colours and mix the rest yourself.

Mix all the colours needed for the design before starting work. To be certain of a successful result, test each colour on a remnant of silk and use the same brand of paint throughout. Do not be concerned if the colours fade as they dry because applying fixer brings back their vibrancy.

5 Start to apply the paint in the middle of a colour area, working out towards the gutta outline. A little colour goes a long way, so take care not to overload the brush. And, as the colour spreads, there is no need to paint right up to the gutta. Stop just short of the outline and let the paint spread up to the edge. Paint the lighter colours in the design first to ensure that if there are any paint runs they can be covered up with a darker colour.

6 Allow the paints to dry thoroughly before removing the silk from the frame and fix the colours according to the manufacturer's instructions for the brand you are using.

Silk 'watercolours'

*Not all silk painting has a rigid outline. You
can paint freehand on to stretched silk or clothing and get the
same dazzling effects that we see in some
watercolour paintings. The secret is to allow shapes and effects
to take their own form as the colours run together.*

In some of the most beautiful watercolour paintings the artist has allowed the wet colours to run into each other and form their own shapes and patterns. These paintings have fluid shapes and no hard lines. Exactly the same is true of 'watercolour' painting on silk.

Forget about making detailed sketches for a painting or using gutta to draw outlines. Instead, paint the design directly on to the stretched silk and allow the colours to work for you. For example, if you paint red on to an area of wet yellow, you will get pools of vivid

△ *Having mastered the basic techniques, why not try your hand at a more ambitious project, like this glorious, hand-painted scarf.*

orange. Take advantage of these spontaneous effects and make them part of the design.

The design

It is important to choose a suitable design for such a loose painting technique. Flowers and plants, flowing abstract shapes and all-over patterns, such as stripes and spots, are all ideal. Avoid patterns with straight edges or subjects with small details.

It is important to allow for the fact that silk dyes spread considerably on fabric. Even when using a special antifusant solution, which helps to stop the dye from sinking into the fabric, the dye will still bleed to some extent — so choose patterns accordingly. The dye will spread less if there is less dye on the brush; so, when painting narrow stripes and stems, use a fine brush and work with just the tips of the bristles.

Large painted areas

Avoid very large, one-colour areas until you are more experienced at silk painting. If it is necessary to have a coloured background, make it deliberately loose and blotchy; alternatively, keep the background area to an absolute minimum by making the main design as large as possible. Wetting the stretched silk first will help the dye to spread more evenly. To avoid brush marks apply the dye with a sponge.

Materials and equipment

For further information on the suitable materials and equipment to use for silk painting — such as paints, dyes and brushes — and for details on how to stretch the silk over a frame before painting, see 'Painting on silk basics'.

Shading

Shadows are easy to do and can make a flat shape look realistic. They are particularly effective for flowers and leaves. Work in two tones — a light and dark mixture of the same colour. Use the light colour to paint the main shape; then, while the dye is still wet, add the darker colour for the shaded parts. The dark tone runs and merges with the light colour to give a soft, natural shading.

'Wet in wet' flowers

1 To start, paint the shape of each flower. Always paint your flower smaller than you actually want it because the dye will run and the shape expand.

2 Add the shading to the centre of the flower by brushing a little of a darker tone of the same colour on to the flower shape. Use the tip of the brush to dot in the stamens at the centre of each flower in a darker colour.

3 This second flower is painted in the same way. The main colour is orange and red has been used for the central shading. Again, the tip of the brush is used to dot in the centre.

Using antifusant

Do not try to be too precise with your design, even when using an antifusant, as you will find there is still a certain amount of spreading when painting.

1 Apply the antifusant solution to the stretched silk with a brush or sponge and allow to dry.

2 The antifusant will seal the surface of the silk and prevent the paint or dye from being absorbed into the fibres of the material.

Silk

The best silk for watercolour painting is pongee. It has a smooth finish and an even weave which doesn't interfere with the flow of the dye. Pongee is available in various thicknesses: the finer grades are used for scarves; cushions and clothing are made of thicker pongee. The thicker the silk, the less the dye spreads.

Thinning agents

Dyes spread more easily if they are thinned; use either water, alcohol or a proprietary thinning agent, depending on the dyes being used. For large areas, just a few drops will give a smoother, flatter effect without weakening the strength of the colour. For pastel shades, add 10 to 90 per cent of thinning agent, depending on how pale the colour needs to be.

Antifusant

The 'watercolour' painting technique is deliberately loose and liquid; for a little more control over the painted shapes, treat the fabric with a special antifusant or anti-spread solution. This seals the silk so that the dyes sit on the surface instead of sinking into the fabric, giving a more clearly defined shape. Apply the solution with a brush or sponge and allow to dry.

Basic technique

There are no hard and fast rules about this type of silk painting. As results cannot be fully controlled, the secret is to allow the blobs of dye to find their own shape and to use them as part of the design.

▷ *This beginner's project shows how the dye spreads — with practice this can be used to your advantage.*

4 For the leaves and stems use a small paint brush: dip only the bristle tips into the dye. The small amount of dye cannot spread, enabling you to paint finer lines and more delicate shapes and patterns.

Textures using alcohol

For simple abstract designs, you can add blobs of alcohol, surgical spirit or denatured alcohol to the dye. The easiest and most effective patterns are created by dabbing on spots of alcohol with a cotton wool swab or with a fine-tipped artists' paint brush.

For a marbled or mottled pattern on a small scale, wait until the dye has dried before adding textures; larger patterns can be created by working on areas of wet colour. Alcohol can also be used in other ways, such as to give flowers pale centres.

Before starting on a larger project, perfect your technique by experimenting on scraps of silk.

1 Paint the background colour on to the stretched silk. If you want to paint a large area, wet the silk first; then apply the dye with a sponge.

2 While the background colour is still damp, dip the cotton wool bud in the alcohol and dab this on to the wet dye.

Silk tie and shorts

For the tie, the design must be free and simple so that any joins in the dye are disguised by the pattern. The stripy design of the boxer shorts is easier and can be continued on the back of the garment.

You will need

◇ White silk boxer shorts
◇ White silk tie
◇ Silk dyes — we used red, yellow, blue and black
◇ Cardboard or plastic sheet
◇ Brushes

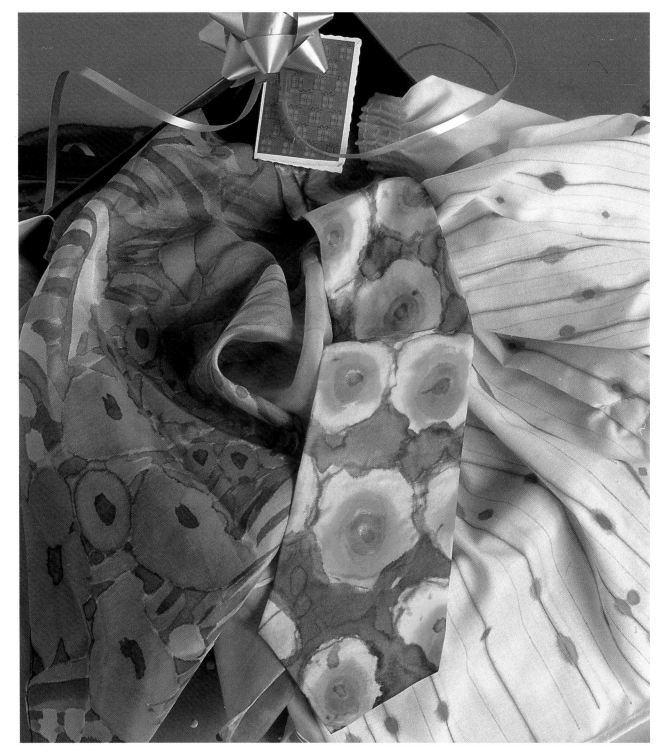

Method

1 When painting ready-made items of clothing, slip a sheet of board or plastic underneath the area you are painting. This stops the silk from seeping through and spoiling the rest of the garment.

2 Mix all the colours to be used before starting to paint, then complete one colour at a time. Wet paint will smudge, so allow the front of the item being painted to dry before turning the garment over to decorate the back.

△ *Here, the colours and patterns of a silk scarf have been used as inspiration for painting the silk tie and boxer shorts. But for an original gift with a personal touch, choose colours and designs to suit the recipient.*

Gold and silver gutta

*Gold and silver gutta offers silk painting
enthusiasts many exciting possibilities. They can be used to
prevent colours blending together, dividing the
shades with a shimmering line, or simply to pattern the silk
with motifs that stay shiny when the fabric is dyed.*

Transparent gutta acts as a resist medium in silk painting, preventing different dyes from merging together so that hard-edged graphic designs are produced. The opaque gutta can be used in the same way but, unlike transparent gutta which disappears when the silk is washed, opaque gutta remains on the surface of the fabric and forms a key part of the design. Opaque gutta is available in many different colours, including metallic gold and silver. The glittering effect of gold or silver can be used to produce striking textile designs.

Metallic gutta can be used in two ways: to separate the cloth into design areas, which can then be coloured in different shades; or, more simply, to add texture to the surface of the cloth with linear

△ *Gold gutta was used to 'draw'
linear patterns on a white top and
scarf. Both were then dyed green.*

designs. The metallic gutta lines will show up against a coloured silk. Alternatively, the design can be drawn in gutta on plain white silk; once the gutta has dried, the silk may be dyed using standard domestic cold water dyes.

Gold-patterned silk

Experiment with gold or silver gutta to produce a simple textile design and make a top or scarf like those shown on the previous page. The light-weight silk used for this project is particularly suitable for clothing as it drapes well. This technique can also be used for furnishing fabrics by substituting a heavier silk or medium-weight cotton as the base fabric.

Here gutta was used to add texture and pattern to the surface of the silk. The linear design was drawn using a gutta applicator, then the silk was dyed a single colour (for small areas the colour can be applied with a sponge). Linear designs work best for this method and they do not have to be complicated — try simple marks, such as dashes, swirls or dots. For multi-coloured designs the placement of the gutta lines must be carefully planned to divide the cloth into sections.

2 Fill the applicator pen with gold gutta. Draw the design on to the fabric, wiping the nib with a tissue before each new start. If you are painting with a single colour you do not need to check for gaps in the outline. Leave the gutta to dry.

▽ *Here silver and gold gutta lines have been placed to prevent the dyes from running into each other.*

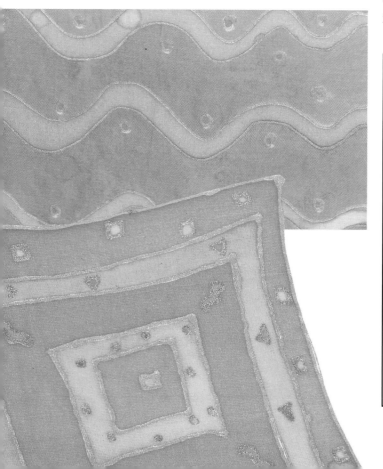

Materials and equipment

For general information on silk painting, in particular gutta and applicators, see 'Painting on silk basics'.

You will need
◇ Length or piece of silk
◇ Frame and silk pins
◇ Gold or silver gutta and applicator with medium nib
◇ Silk paint (or cold water dye) and fixer
◇ Paint brush or sponge

1 Stretch the silk across a frame and secure with silk pins. Run your hand over the silk to make sure there are no dips or ridges, as the surface needs to be smooth and taut for the gutta to work — if necessary, adjust the pins.

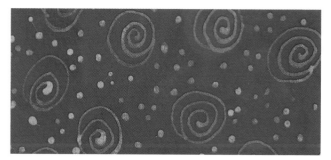

3 Using a sponge or a large paint brush, apply the silk paint to the fabric. Work fairly quickly to prevent streaks or uneven patches of colour forming. Leave the paint to dry thoroughly. Alternatively, remove the silk from the frame and use a suitable cold water dye to colour the silk; leave to dry.

4 If you used the first method to paint the silk, now remove the silk from the frame. Fix the dye following the manufacturer's instructions.

TIP ◇ WASHING & AFTERCARE

◇ Protect your ironing board with a cloth to prevent the gold and silver marking it when you iron the silk to fix the colours.

◇ Coloured gutta will not stand up to frequent washing and ironing. Dry cleaning may remove the gold and silver.

◇ Wash silk in medium hot water and mild soap flakes. Take care to rinse thoroughly as any soap left behind will mark the silk.

◇ Always allow silk to drip dry. Do not wring out wet silk or put in a tumble dryer as this will damage the fibres.

◇ If you are not going to use the silk immediately, wrap it in polythene or acid-free tissue paper and store in a dry place.

Batik dyeing

*The craft of batik dyeing comes from Java,
where for centuries the islanders have created beautiful fabrics
using this traditional melted wax technique.
Today the craft is practised all over the world and many of the
original Javanese designs are still in use.*

Batik is a fabric dyeing technique in which melted wax is painted or drawn on to fabric and allowed to dry before the fabric is immersed in the dye solution. The waxed areas resist the colour and remain undyed. When the wax is removed, the protected areas often have an attractive and characteristic 'crinkled' appearance where the wax has cracked and allowed the dye to seep through.

Batik fabrics are unique and they can be put to practical use and made into clothes, cushion covers, aprons, table cloths and wall hangings.

Simple batik designs can be made easily by applying the wax with an artist's brush. For more intricate patterns and to create the authentic swirling decorations familiar in traditional batik work, you will need a special wax-filled pen called a tjanting.

◁ *A combination of strong colours and bold designs applied using the tried and tested method of batik resist dyeing, is used to stunning effect on this traditional garment.*

▽ *Batik designs often take their subjects from nature, but the techniques involved mean that once images are broken down into distinct areas of colour they may take on an abstract appearance.*

Brush batik

Many modern batik dyers use a brush to apply the melted wax because it is easier to control than a tjanting. Dip the brush in the melted wax and leave it there for a few seconds. Remove any surplus wax by squeezing the brush against the sides of the pan, then transfer the wax to the fabric. Because of the rapidly drying nature of the wax you will find it necessary to dip the brush into the wax fairly frequently. Use a cloth or a newspaper to catch any drips.

Tjanting batik

Many traditional batiks, recognizable by their intricate, linear detail, are made with a tjanting — a small cup with a spout set on the end of a handle — which is dipped into the molten wax. The wax is then trickled over the fabric.

Tools and equipment

Batik materials are surprisingly simple. For the dyeing you will need a dyebath, a jug or bowl, and rubber gloves for mixing the dye.

There are some extra materials needed specifically for batik work.

Wax

Special batik wax, available from craft shops, is the most convenient because it is ready to use and has exactly the right degree of flexibility for batik work. Wax from ordinary melted-down candles usually proves too flaky when used on its own, but beeswax can be used on its own. The best combination, is to mix paraffin wax, which most candles are made from, with beeswax: use 70 per cent paraffin wax and 30 per cent beeswax.

Double saucepan

Wax must be melted in a double saucepan, otherwise it can overheat dangerously. A good alternative is to use a small pot or tin can inside a larger pan of boiling water. Whether you use the real thing or the improvised version, it is important to make sure the water is constantly topped up and is not allowed to boil dry.

Fabrics

For best results, choose natural fibres, such as cotton, linen and silk — the traditional fabrics for batik dyeing. If you use synthetic material, do a test piece first. Results can be disappointing and, depending on the fabric and dye, are usually much paler.

All fabrics must be washed to remove any dressing.

Dyes

Use cold water dye or a craft dye, following the manufacturer's instructions. Hot water dyes cannot be used because the heat melts the wax. If you are using more than one colour, check the effect of overdyeing before starting. Usually paler colours are used first, and then darker colours added.

Wooden frame

You will find it easier to apply the wax if the fabric is stretched across a frame and secured with thumbtacks. Either make your own from four pieces of wood or – provided it is the right size – use an old wooden picture frame.

Tjanting

Available from arts and crafts shops and from specialist suppliers, a tjanting is the traditional tool for drawing lines with melted wax. It has a tube-like nib and a reservoir for the wax, which enables you to make a regular, continuous line without constantly dipping it in to the wax. Some tjantings have double or even triple nibs, enabling you to make two or three lines at a time.

Brushes

For broad, undulating lines and flat areas, a good quality artist's brush is ideal for applying melted wax. Choose a suitable size and texture for the effect required.

Charcoal and craft knife

For the initial drawing you will need either a piece of charcoal, chalk or a soft pencil. You will also need a craft knife or utility knife to score the wax prior to dyeing.

Using a tjanting

A tjanting requires practice, but basically you must trail the nib across the fabric to produce dots and a variety of continuous lines. To refill a tjanting, dip the reservoir into the melted wax. To stop a tjanting line go back along the line you have just made, then slip a card or plastic lid under the nib to stop the flow of wax.

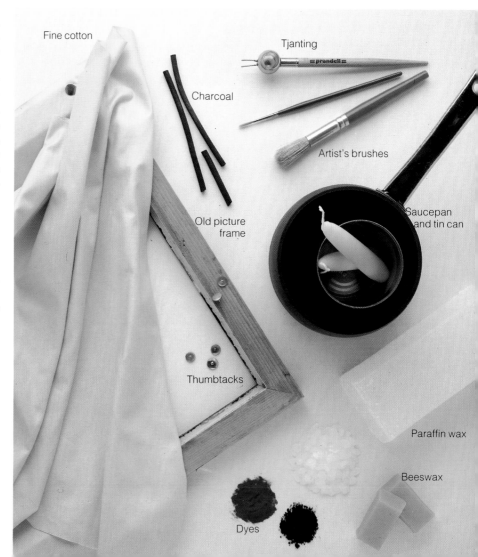

Fine cotton
Tjanting
Charcoal
Artist's brushes
Old picture frame
Saucepan and tin can
Thumbtacks
Paraffin wax
Beeswax
Dyes

◆ TIP   **THE WAX DESIGN**

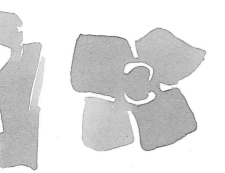

When applying melted wax to your drawn design, you can choose whether you want the shapes or the background to be coloured. In the diagram on the far left, the flower has been waxed out and it is the background that is coloured. In the near left diagram the background has been waxed to create a coloured flower.

How to batik

1 First you must sketch your design on to a piece of fabric, using either charcoal or a soft pencil. When you have drawn your design, stretch the fabric across a wooden frame or an old picture frame and fix it firmly in position with thumbtacks.

2 Prepare the wax by melting it in a double boiler. Wax must not be overheated and should be removed from the heat before it starts to smoke. Test the wax on a piece of fabric. The painted wax should be transparent. If it looks opaque and white, it has probably not penetrated and is not hot enough. To avoid drips of hot wax, place the container as close as possible to your working hand.

3 Following the drawn lines, fill in the design with the melted wax. Use a brush for wide lines and large areas, and a tjanting for fine lines. You must work quickly because wax cools rapidly and needs to be reheated.

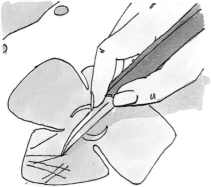

4 If you have large waxed areas in your design it is a good idea to add extra texture by scratching into the wax with a sharp knife or scalpel blade. This lets a small amount of dye seep through and avoids areas of unbroken colour.

5 When the waxing and texturing are complete, you are ready to start dyeing. Remove the cloth from the frame and crunch it up a little to encourage hairline cracks. Then dye the fabric in the dyebath, following the manufacturer's instructions.

6 Before applying a second and subsequent colours, hang the fabric to dry without removing the wax. Do not wring or apply heat. When dry, decide which areas are to be overdyed and either remove the wax (see step 7) and apply a new layer to the areas to be masked for the second colour, or apply further wax in addition to the first waxing. Dye the fabric by immersing it in the second colour.

7 Repeat this process for further colours. To remove the wax from the finished batik, place the fabric between two sheets of newspaper and iron with a hot iron until the wax melts. An alternative method is to boil the fabric in water to melt the wax. Finally, wash the batik carefully, then dry and iron in the normal way.

DESIGN LIBRARY

Batik designs

When it comes to deciding what to use for your basic design there are numerous possibilities. The different finishes achieved with the tjanting and a brush immediately give you the scope to use delicate, flowing lines or to cover larger, more defined areas. As a result of the effects achieved with wax, linear, swirling forms from nature such as plants, birds and fish are traditionally popular. You can choose to repeat a single motif over and over again, or opt for one large image that covers the entire fabric.

There is no need to be daunted by the thought of coming up with your own designs for batik dyeing. In fact, you are not necessarily tied to using original ideas at all. It is possible to lift or adapt designs from almost anywhere, not only from other fabrics, but from any item that might carry a suitable decoration from wallpaper and crockery to wrapping paper and ceramic tiles.

◁ *A linear pattern works as a frame for freehand designs.*

△ *The freehand swirls that link this design are typical of what can be achieved using a tjanting.*

△ *The irregular application of wax gives batik its spontaneous and undisciplined look.*

Batik techniques

*One of the pleasures of using the batik technique
to dye fabrics is to build up the layers of colour to produce a
rich pattern. This process takes a little more
skill and patience than one-colour batik, but it is much more
challenging and rewarding to try.*

Develop your batik skills with the simple project overpage, which explains step-by-step how to produce a pattern with four colours. The key to achieving a successful pattern with a range of clear, crisp colours is to plan — not just the placement of colours — but the order in which they will be dyed. The colour must be built from light to dark, as light colours cannot be dyed over dark ones.

▽ *Striking, abstract designs can be achieved using traditional methods.*

Choosing the fabric

The background colour of the fabric can be incorporated into the design, or completely covered with colour. White fabric is the best choice for a beginner as the colours of the dyes will not be distorted and, provided the wax is applied thoroughly, the colours will be true. White fabric must also be used if the finished design includes white areas or lines.

Coloured fabrics can be used but they will affect the final look of the dyes and they must be pale or clear enough to allow the dyes to show up. Bright yellow, for instance, could be dyed with blue or red but basic colour theory will apply and you will end up with green from the blue dye and a lighter looking red, or even orange, from the red dye. Obviously, using a coloured background fabric offers a lot of potential for experimentation, but the results are unpredictable unless you are an experienced batik artist.

Neutrals like beige, off-white, pale grey and ecru can be used, but these too will affect the final colour scheme, causing the colours to look muddied or reduced.

Suitable dyes

The best dyes to use for batik are cold water dyes, as the wax will melt in hot dye. Special batik dyes — procion mix reactive dyes — are available from art and craft shops. They come in powder form together with a fixing bath. Dylon cold water dyes are also suitable.

Procion mix reactive dyes These extremely fast, cold water reactive dyes give brilliant colour to cotton, linen and viscose fabrics as well as to silk and wool. Dyeing with them is a simple and magical process. The brilliance and fastness of these dyes makes them the most popular for teachers of batik and craftspersons alike.

Fixing method The paints come with a fixative bath powder which has to be mixed with water. For the best results, follow the manufacturer's instructions for use.

Sequence of colour

When planning a batik design it is important to consider what will happen when colours are overdyed and to incorporate this feature into the design. Being able to anticipate exactly what will happen if a certain colour is dyed over another can only be gained with experience;

try overdyeing a few swatches of fabric before making a choice of dyes. Dip the sample into the dyes in the order you plan to use them to test the result. For future reference, note down the dyes and the order in which they were used.

Designing your own batik patterns should be a lot of fun and, provided you are happy to experiment, you will come up with some unexpected and pleasing results.

Transferring designs

If you are confident and have a steady hand you can apply the wax directly on to the fabric without marking out the design first. However, for a more controlled design, it is better to trace the pattern on to the fabric. Keep the designs and outlines simple — you will find that even basic patterns produce very attractive results.

Alternative method

If you find you enjoy batik dyeing, try removing the wax after each application. It is rather messy but with this method the colours can be planned and you will not have to worry about overdyeing unless you want to make it an extra feature of the pattern. For example, start with a piece of white fabric and paint wide stripes in wax. Dye it red. Remove the wax, then cover the red areas and some of the white stripes with a new application of wax. Then dye the cloth with yellow. When the wax has been removed again the result should be red, yellow and white stripes. This method can be used for any pattern.

Leaf pattern fabric

A pure white cotton was chosen as the background fabric for this design — although the white is hardly apparent in the finished pattern. The colours were built up by overdyeing from the lightest shade, turquoise. The white lines were marked first, then the fabric dyed turquoise. Next the leaf shapes were waxed in and the next colour, pink, added. Note how the pink comes out a mauve shade when dyed over the turquoise. The pink areas were splattered with wax and the fabric dyed with blue.

You will need

◇ Fine, closely woven white cotton (white silk could also be used)
◇ Batik wax, made from 75 per cent paraffin and 25 per cent

<table>
<tr><td>◇ TIP</td><td>TEXTURE</td></tr>
</table>

Create the crazed line effect, typical of batik, by crushing large areas of wax before they are dyed. Note that if you are forcing the fabric into a small dye bath, this may happen anyway.

microcrystalline
◇ ICI procion mix reactive dye in turquoise, pink and royal blue
◇ Tjantung tool
◇ Household or hogshair brush, for applying the wax
◇ Fine brush for applying colour
◇ Strong saucepan and smaller bowl or a purpose-built wax pot with thermostat or electric ring
◇ Wooden frame
◇ Dye-bath: a baby bath is ideal
◇ Rubber gloves
◇ Thumbtacks
◇ Masking tape
◇ 4B pencil
◇ Iron
◇ Absorbent paper towels

Preparation

1 Before you start, boil the fabric in soapy water to make sure that it will successfully absorb the

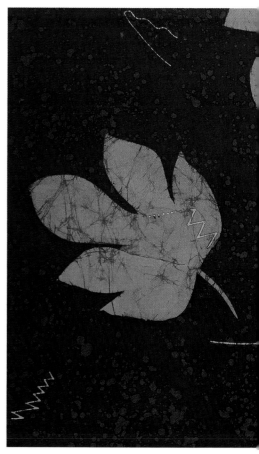

dye. Leave to dry, then iron the fabric and stretch it on to a frame. Secure the fabric in place with thumbtacks.

2 Put the wax into a pot and gradually heat to about 248°F (120°C). Keep the wax at this temperature so that it will evenly penetrate the fabric to form a resist. If the wax is too cool it will not run or repel the dye. Alternatively, the wax can get out of control if it is too hot. Place the wax pot in a handy position near to the frame and place some protective paper underneath it.

Working the design

1 Fill the tjanting tool with molten wax by dipping it into the pot; hold for a few seconds and

then remove the half-filled cup. Using absorbent paper towels, wipe off excess wax from the outside of the cup.

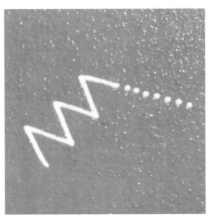

2 Draw random wax lines to reserve areas of white design. Work quickly and rhythmically, and regularly refill the tjanting with fresh molten wax.

3 Dye the fabric using the turquoise colour. Wear rubber gloves and carefully follow the manufacturer's instructions.

▽ *The leaf motif, in clear turquoise, stands out in the completed fabric. The white lines were marked in wax with a tjanting.*

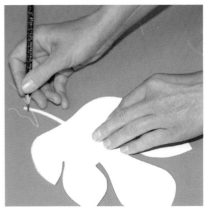

4 Position leaf stencil on cloth and draw around it using the pencil. Repeat over rest of the cloth, changing the position of the stencil and making sure that the leaf will point in different directions for a random effect.

△ *The first three samples (from the top) show white fabric dyed with turquoise, royal blue and pink — the colours are clear and true. The fourth sample shows white fabric dyed turquoise, then overdyed pink. The fifth sample shows all three colours overdyed.*

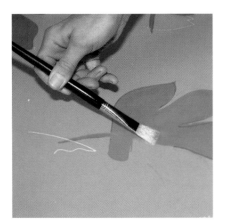

5 Using pencil outline as guide, fill solid shape with wax using a stiff, natural hair brush to give consistent resist to cloth.

6 Overdye the turquoise colour with pink dye to obtain mauve. The overdyeing only affects the exposed areas of the design — the already waxed white and turquoise areas are completely protected from the new colour.

7 After thoroughly air drying the fabric, place the masking tape diagonally and at regular intervals on to the cloth. Using a large, wax-filled brush, splatter the wax down gently over the whole cloth. Remove the masking tape. To add more texture to the solid leaf shapes, gently crack the wax by crushing it in your hand; this will enable the dye to make a marbled pattern on the surface.

8 Dye the fabric using the royal blue dye. The spattered background effect and clear stripe will be immediately apparent.

9 Hang the fabric outside to dry and fix the colours. The final, royal blue colour highlights the traditional overdyeing sequences from light to dark. This process is the most common and distinctive form of batik dyeing.

Using different coloured base fabrics

◁ *It is possible to use a coloured base fabric for batik, however the dyes will come out a different colour. For instance, the bright yellow cloth (top) was dyed with the same pink and royal blue shades used for the project, but the final colours produced are startlingly different. The pink, dyed over yellow, produces a subtle orange shade, while the royal blue goes quite green. The plum colour was produced by overdyeing both blue and pink.*

▷ *If a cream fabric, or other neutral shade, is used as the base cloth the colours of the dyes will be fairly true. As with the yellow sample, the cream was dyed with pink and royal blue, and then both colours in succession. When compared with the swatches on the previous page, which were dyed on white, the colours are only slightly distorted.*

Finishing off

1 Substantial amounts of wax can be removed from the cloth by ironing it between sheets of absorbent paper. The remainder can be removed by dry cleaning or boiling out.

2 Rinse fabric in running water to remove excess colour and then wash it in hot soapy water. This will return the cloth to its natural texture. Iron the fabric.

TIP	WAX

If necessary, touch up all of the previously waxed areas as you work to prevent the colours from being ruined by the next dye colour.

INDEX